Painting Animals
in Watercolour

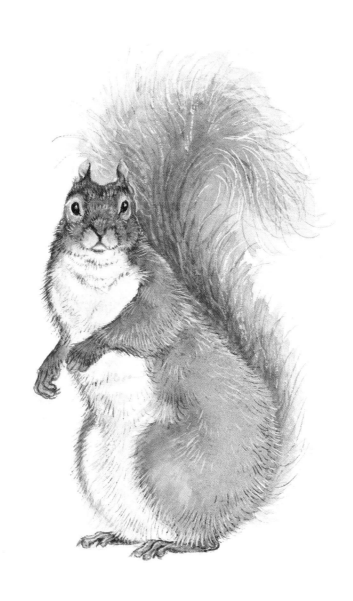

Painting Animals in Watercolour

SALLY MICHEL

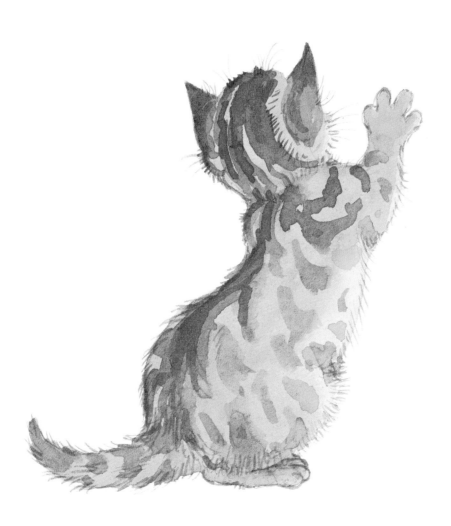

SEARCH PRESS LIMITED

First published in 1985

by Search Press Ltd.,
Wellwood, North Farm Road,
Tunbridge Wells, Kent TN2 3DR

Copyright © Search Press Limited 1985

Reprinted 1989

First published in paperback 1989

Text, drawings and paintings by Sally Michel
Design by David Stanley

ISBN 0 85532 555 0 (C)
ISBN 0 85532 648 4 (Pb)

Made and printed in Spain by Artes Graphicas Elkar, S. Coop.
Autonomía, 71 - 48012-Bilbao - Spain. - D. L. BI-226-82

CONTENTS

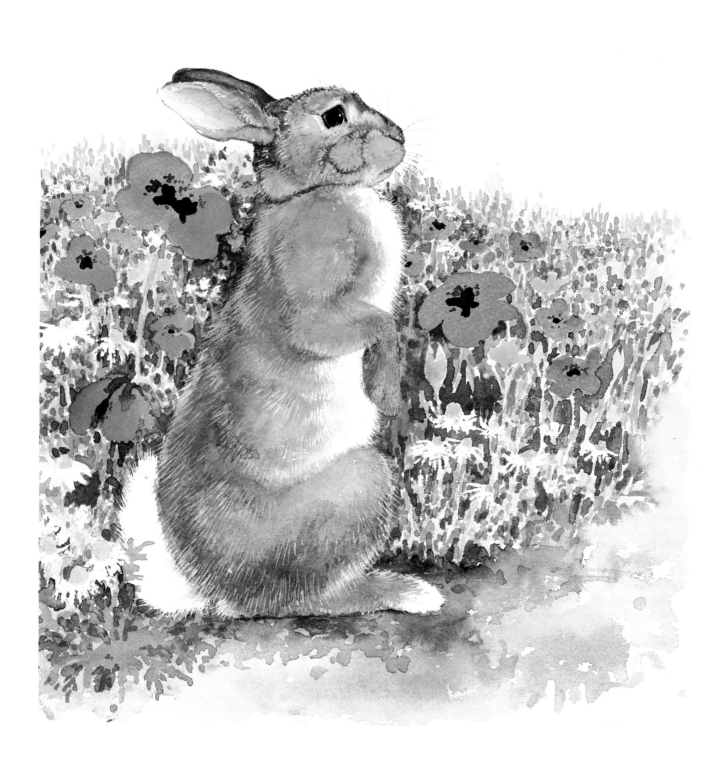

INTRODUCTION

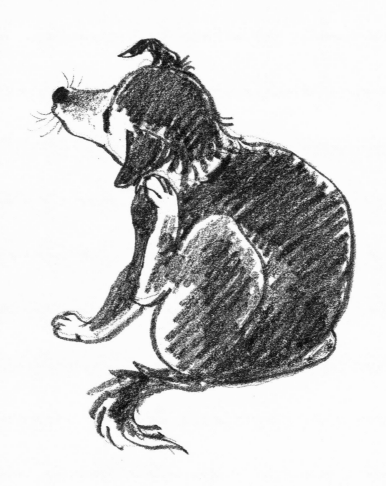

Introduction

One essential difference between painting or drawing animals, and painting or drawing other subjects – landscape, still life, plants, or buildings, or even a human portrait – is that, while most of these stay reasonably still, animals move. It is impossible to know, when you start to draw a motionless and apparently somnolent animal, whether you will have time for a detailed, leisurely, considered study, or will need to work very fast to sketch its general appearance.

Another difference is that a subjective approach, appropriate to most other subjects, will in the case of animal painting, probably defeat its own object. There is no point in painting an animal if you are not going to present its essential character, whether in near-photographic detail or as a swiftly observed and recorded impression. This requires considerable accuracy – for if the structure is not right, your drawing will not be of that animal. This is not to say that careful observation and accurate drawing are less important for other subjects, but there is more scope for choice, and selection; for instance, a tree in a landscape or an awkward spray of leaves in a flower painting, can be moved to improve the composition; and television aerials and parked cars can be omitted from the picture of a half-timbered thatched cottage. All this is permissible, even desirable. But, with animals, alteration may mean that you have created a new animal or misrepresented an existing one.

Even the apparently random patches of colour on a tortoiseshell cat obey certain rules; the positions of feet depend on the position of the other parts of the animal; obviously some changes can be made, but enormous care must be taken that there is a good reason for each of them. The danger of making arbitrary alterations is greater with wild animals than it is with domestic pets. If you change the pattern on a giraffe shown in a particular landscape, you may be transporting a different variety many hundreds of miles from its native habitat, and making its camouflage ineffectual in addition!

However, for most of us more opportunities arise for drawing and painting domestic animals, and experience gained from working on these can be applied to any other creatures we may become interested in.

This book begins with a discussion of the general approach to the subject; what to do, how to start, and what to use; how to reconcile ability with ambition, maintain enjoyment and avoid discouragement.

Next, the range of accessible subjects. I make no apology for including a large section on dogs, which are so varied in size and shape; cats, the other principal sharers of our home life, also have a chapter of their own.

I then look at birds and those small creatures which live in our homes in a less intimate relationship – for example, gerbils, guinea pigs, hamsters, and fish.

Finally we turn to horses, and other creatures to be seen outside our homes, in gardens, the countryside, parks and zoos, both as subjects of portraits, and as elements in a larger scene.

It is likely that anyone interested in the subject of animal painting in a specific medium already has some familiarity with that medium; so it seems superfluous to expatiate on the character and qualities of watercolour or to give long lists of pigments, and describe the available brushes, papers etc., except in regard to the particular requirements of the painting of animals. It may be worth emphasizing, however, that it is desirable to use materials of good quality, and to pay attention to the permanence of pigments chosen; the more expensive 'Artist's' watercolours go further than cheaper grades, though even they vary in permanence, earth colours being among the most stable. Good brushes last longer than inferior ones, but sable can be prohibitively high in price; good quality nylon brushes can be excellent, beautifully springy when new, although some have a tendency to change suddenly into a kind of miniature flue brush. However the larger sizes are so much cheaper than their sable equivalents that one or two are worth buying; they are harder than sable, but this may be preferable to some of the other less expensive large wash brushes in squirrel or pony hair, which are very floppy and soft. It is a matter of personal preference.

The particular requirements for animal work are:
1. Plenty of paper for preliminary drawings; you need to be able to use it without worrying about the cost, as it is desirable to record every movement and position of the animal, to refer to when making your picture;
2. A small light drawing board; a piece of plywood, about 12in. × 16in. (30cm × 40cm) is a good size, and useful when pursuing a reluctant model as it retreats from view, or takes up a position behind furniture from which it can keep an eye on you and your questionable activities;
3. One or two really fine brushes, O, or OO, for the details of hair and whiskers;
4. If you intend to paint mammals, such colours as will permit you to mix a wide range of browns, from pale yellowish, reddish, to dark; this, in effect, means much the same palette as for most other subjects, but with perhaps a larger choice of browns. As with any medium of painting, it is a good idea to start with a small selection of six to eight pigments, and add to these if you find a lack of any colour. You need everything you might want for landscape, as the backgrounds of your animals will often be precisely that.

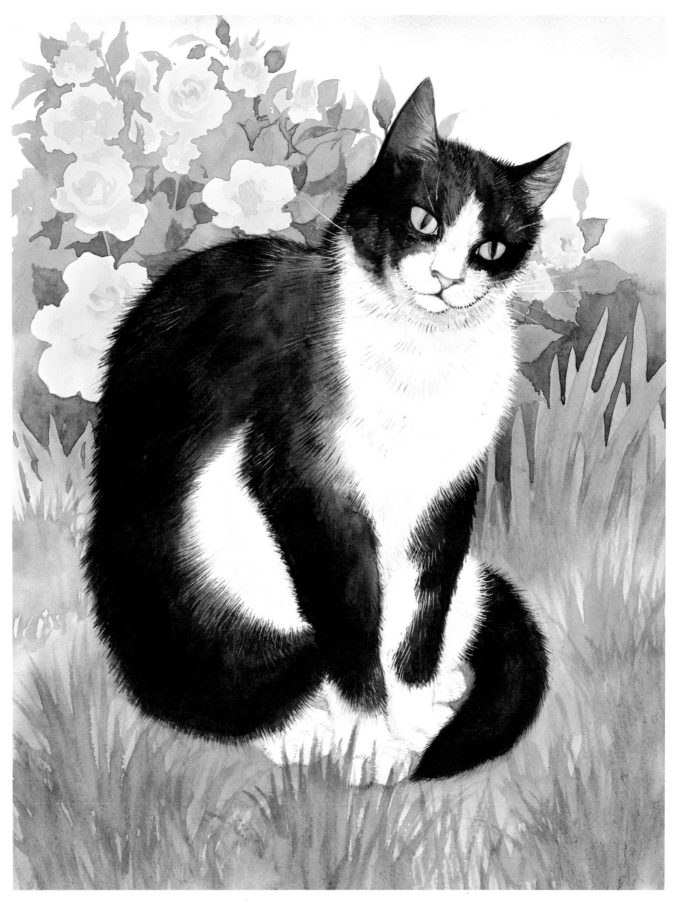

Colours and treatment

I find that the colours I use most are:
Yellow ochre;
Burnt sienna;
a very sharp lemon-yellow (Winsor yellow or Cadmium lemon);
Lamp black;
Phthalocyanine blue;
Payne's grey.

Some others which are almost equally essential, but used in smaller amounts, are:
Cadmium red light;
Quinacridone pink (permanent rose) for tongues, noses and toes, particularly for white or very young animals;
a deeper yellow – Cadmium (*not* chrome yellow which fades);
French Ultramarine;
Winsor violet – particularly useful for the more subtle browns of fur and feathers.

Incidentally, when you are painting tropical birds or fish, their brilliance is such that it may be necessary to use specially bought colours.

The pictures on pages 10–13 show some different approaches, ranging in complexity, from the very simple black and white cat to the peacock butterfly on page 12; the cat is little more than a one-colour wash drawing, with small additions for the features; the hedgehog was first drawn in pencil with added washes, and the hen drawn in pen, with wash added. The squirrel is built up in loose wet washes on wet paper, with sharpened up details and many hairs added with a fine brush; the badger is treated in much the same way, but in a simpler, broader, style.

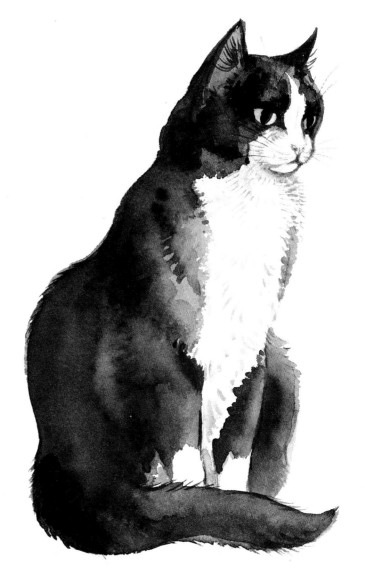

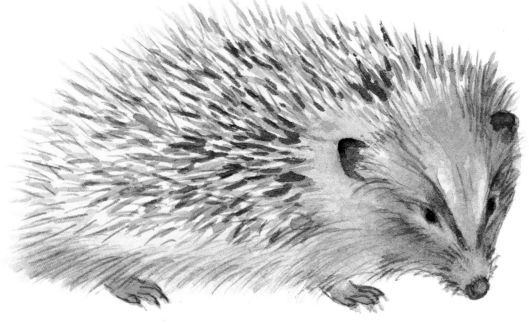

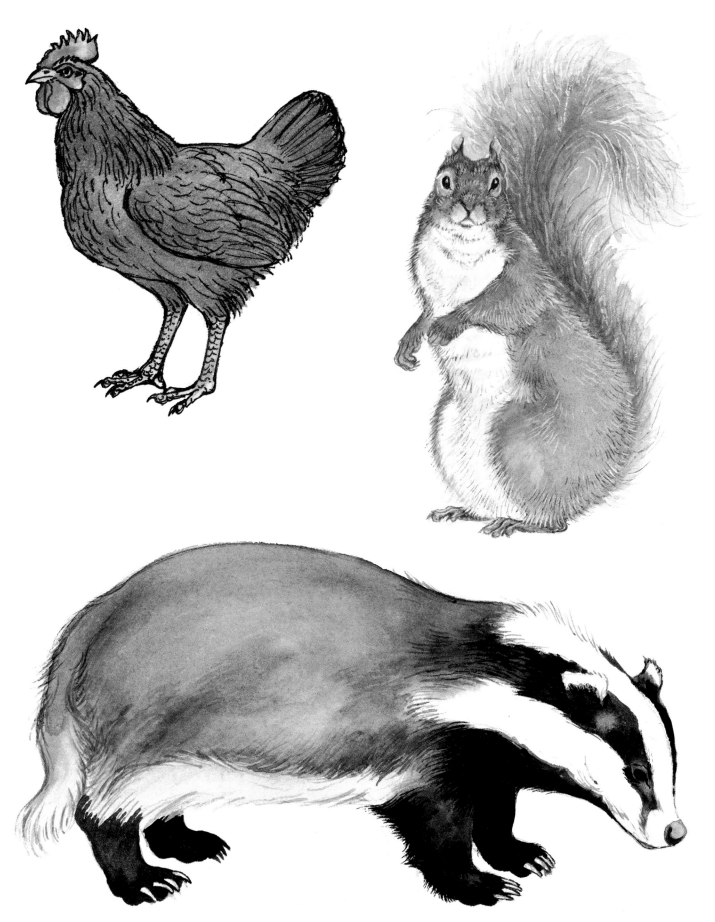

Watercolour techniques

The pony was built up with wet wash, one part at a time; when these were dry, the parts were co-ordinated with a pale wash that preserved the definition and gave an impression of the glossy nature of the pony's hide. The tail, mane, and grass were added, still as separate patches of colour, to complete the figure.

The peacock butterfly is the most complex of these drawings, both the insect itself and the stonecrop on which it has settled. The nature of the butterfly's markings demands a detailed and realistic treatment, and this dictates the style of the flower, which needs to be consistent with the rest.

The treatment used for the fox is fairly complicated, combining elements of those used in the badger and pony sketches. It is a particularly useful treatment for animals, and is employed in many of the pictures on this book. I show here some of my previous fox sketches which helped me in building up the picture.

These pictures are here to illustrate techniques. They are not necessarily the most suitable subjects for a

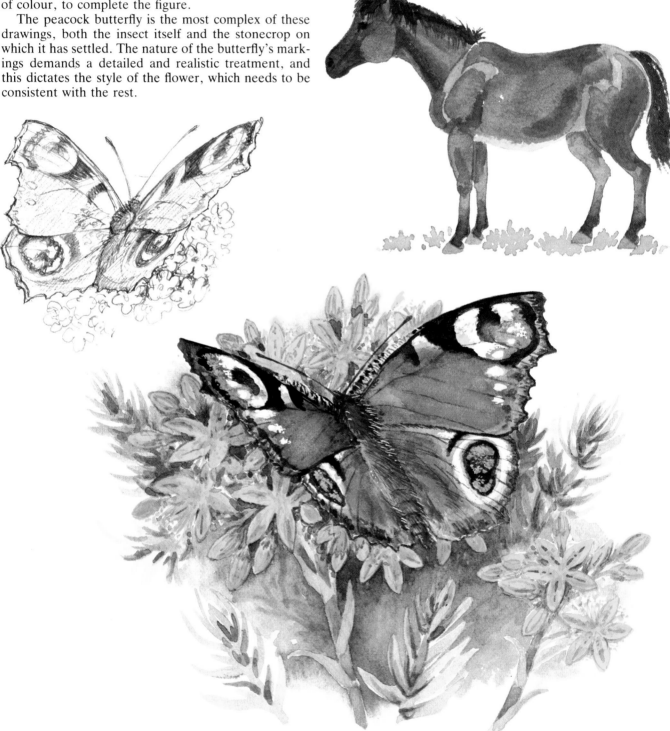

beginner to start with, but, because of the inherent problem of a moving model, it is sensible to start with a sleeping subject. It may not stay asleep, and even if it does, it may still move; but the chances are that there will be periods when you can proceed uninterrupted.

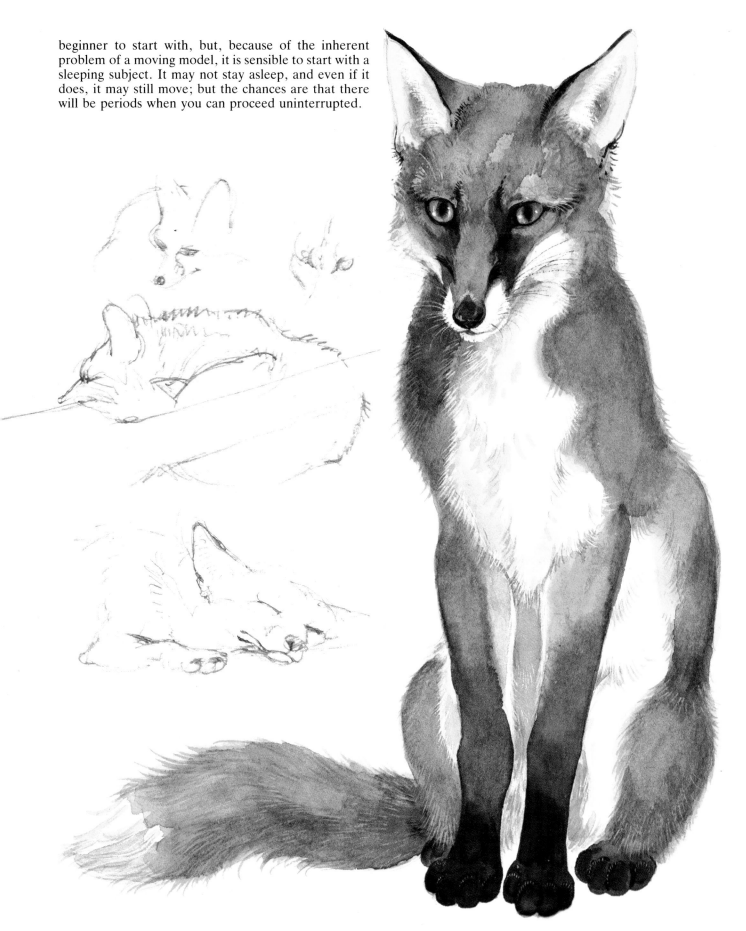

Drawings of a sleeping animal (dog)

Sleeping dogs: *the drawings on these two pages, the product of one session, show how even a sleeping dog can provide a variety of poses.*

Whatever medium is intended for carrying out a painting, it must start with drawing. After years of experience, an artist may base his picture on a sketch so apparently slight that it seems almost as if the drawing stage is being by-passed. For this to be done successfully, careful study and observation must have been carried out in the past, over many years, so that the artist's thorough stored knowledge of the subject enables him to sum up very quickly the essential facts of the model before him, and to add these to what is already in his memory, to produce a true and completely understood presentation of what is there. Until this study has been done, it is as well to spend as much time as you can on drawing, and on the careful exploratory looking which is its necessary preliminary and accompaniment. Even if you have no immediate intention of doing a painting, no time spent on drawing is wasted; carry a sketch book with you, and draw whenever possible. Practice in drawing, on any subject, increases your ability to draw any other subject, so that even if the result appears to be of little significance, it has a beneficial effect on your general ability. By filling sketch books with drawings of many different animals you are building up your knowledge of their structure and habits, and also a useful record to refer to for later work. Do not be disheartened at the apparent impossibility of completing any one drawing – even the smallest sketch can be useful. Start another drawing if your subject moves – you may well later have a chance to go back to the first one. Keep all your drawings, however incomplete; make written notes about colours, behaviour, the age and sex of the animal and anything else that contributes to your knowledge. Label and date all your drawings, not forgetting to include the year. Try to draw from different viewpoints, and pay attention to the structure of eyes, feet, and ears.

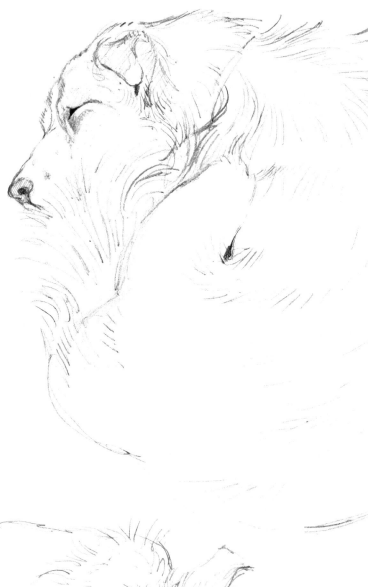

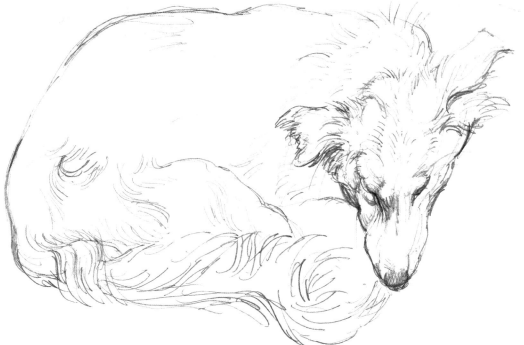

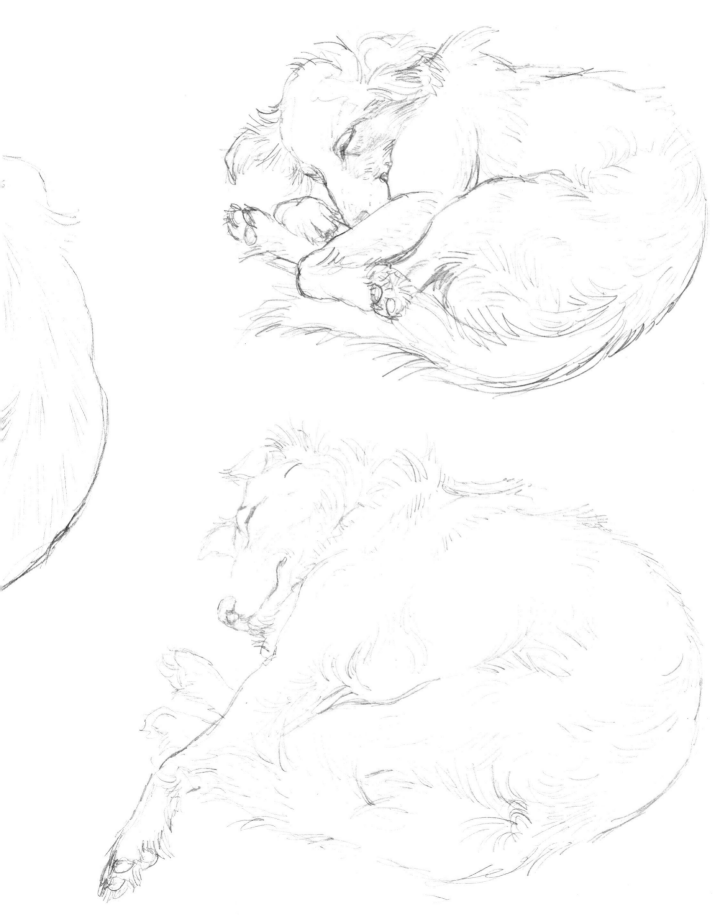

Eyes, ears, feet, and hoofs

It is essential when drawing and painting animals to have some knowledge of the principles of the structure of certain features and details. This enables the artist to draw them with understanding; and it permits comparison with those features in different animals, to perceive in what ways they are the same, and in what they differ.

Eyes, for instance, are in all vertebrates more or less spherical, which means that the surface of the visible part of the eye is curved. The part of the eye which is not visible affects the shape of the face around the eye, and it can often be seen where these forms continue the rounded shape of the whole eye, where bone forms a protective curve around it, and where eyelids follow its shape.

The visible part of the eye is not always the same: humans show quite a lot of the white part outside the coloured iris; but dogs and cats little or none. Gorillas have black 'whites' to their eyes; while owls' eyes are so large that the two very nearly touch inside their heads. Humans and dogs have round pupils; cats' pupils are vertical slits, and those of goats and sheep horizontal; all these facts, when correctly depicted, contribute to the convincing effect of a picture.

Ears, also, are more complicated than the triangular flap they often appear to be; the flap is only the top part of the ear, and quite complicated shapes can be seen at the rear side of the base of the flap, though fortunately perhaps it is sometimes partly hidden by fur. The hair growing inside and around the ear also deserves careful examination and, when it is well understood and drawn, it helps to give a picture the right character. In fact this applies to hair patterns in general – their inclusion adds interest and authenticity to a picture, but they must be understood if they are included, for depicting them inaccurately is worse than leaving them out. This applies to any feature of a painting; omit what you do not want to include, but do not put in something that is not there.

Feet can also be a source of difficulty. It is often difficult to tell how many toes an animal or bird has, particularly as they are frequently half-buried in fur or feathers. It helps to be able to handle the animal, but this is not always advisable or possible; also, to look at and draw museum specimens is useful for such information, but remember to allow for their rather stiff and shrunken state. Birds' feet are difficult, and the arrangement of the toes when perching can be obscure – one or two can be seen, but it is not always clear whether all the others are at the back of the foot, or merely hidden by feathers. One may feel that, if they cannot be seen it does not matter, but it is still true that the knowledge helps one to draw the parts one can see with greater understanding.

At first sight a *hoof* is not like the conventional foot with four or five toes, since it has changed over the millennia to fit the way of life of a running animal, whose life depends on its being able to run faster and further than the carnivorous owners of paws, claws, and cutting teeth. However, it makes more sense when it is realised that the hoof is the one remaining toe in horses, or two in cattle, pigs and other cloven hoofed animals, with greatly enlarged and strengthened toe-nails, which keep a hoofed animal literally 'on its toes', ready to run and keep running from danger.

The drawings of some of these features on page 17 are done in a fairly detailed way; this degree of finish is obviously not always going to be wanted in a picture, but the structure needs to be understood, however impressionistic the rendering of it may be. It is remarkable how a drawing which shows very little specific detail can still manage to convey the complete structure, so long as the artist has himself been aware of that structure; there is a magic in an apparently random scribble or brush mark by one who knows and has observed the form, for it implies the whole underlying structure without apparently defining it at all.

Fur, feathers and hair
(*see also page 18*)

Texture of fur, hair and plumage can be conveyed in many different ways in watercolour. The different treatments employed will depend on the character of the paper used, the speed with which the picture is to be done, the scale of the picture as a whole, and of the animal being painted within the picture.

The examples on this page show possible ways of conveying long and short, fluffy, shaggy and smooth hair and feathers. There are other ways to do it, some of which will be seen in the illustrations throughout the book, but however one is working, one point to keep in mind is that the shinier the subject, the greater the difference in tone between the darkest and the lightest parts, and the more sharply they are divided – a shiny surface reflects light, and on those parts where there is no light reflected, the tone is very dark. Similarly, the finer the size of the individual hairs, the less they can be seen as separate objects; so that fine hairs may be shown either as the smallest of brush marks, or left out, although it is permissible to put in a few to indicate hair-growth.

To show a fluffy or woolly character of fur or down, the paper may be wetted with clean water, and the wash allowed to spread to give a soft indefinite edge; if a coarsely woolly or shaggy look is needed, whole locks of hair can be done in this way; the cloudier the look required, the more general the application of colour.

A velvety texture to some extent combines the characteristics of a smooth shiny surface and a fine, fluffy one; it seems logical therefore, to portray it with a considerable difference between its darkest and lightest tones, but with no sharp change from one to the other, as with a smooth all-over wash, darkening in tone fairly suddenly, but very smoothly.

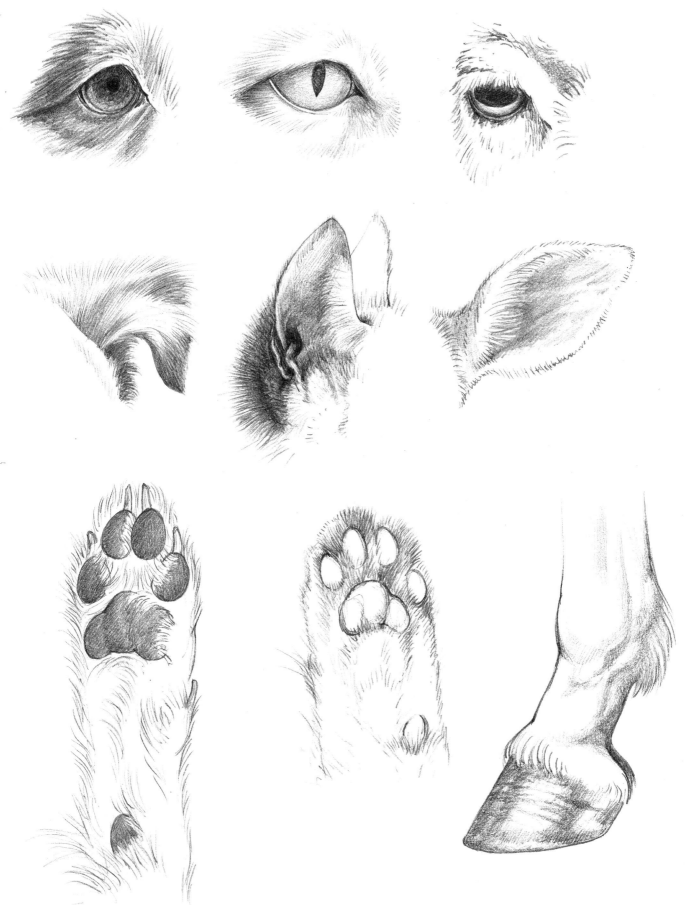

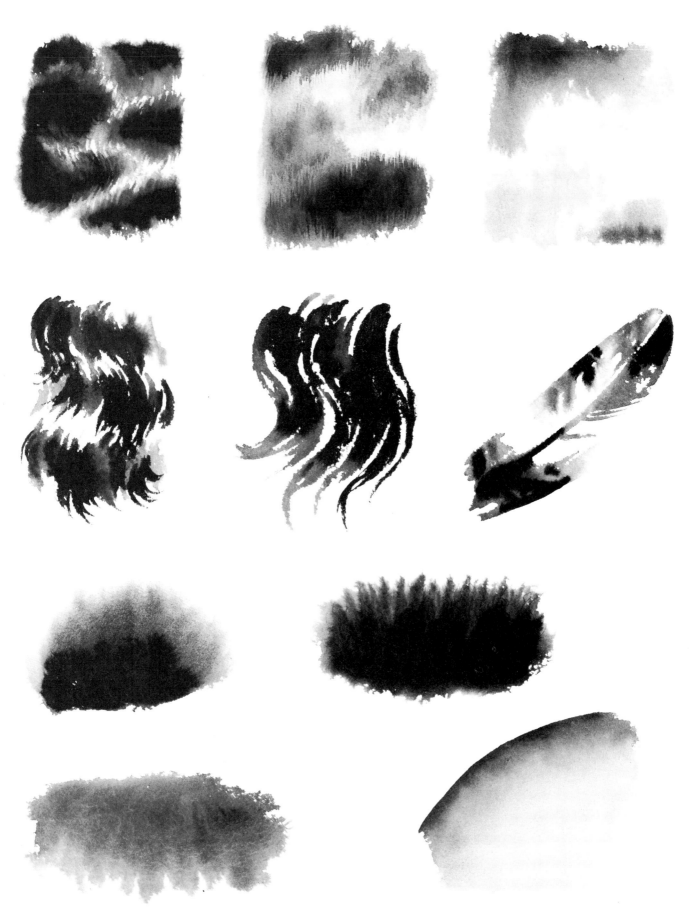

ANIMALS
IN REPOSE

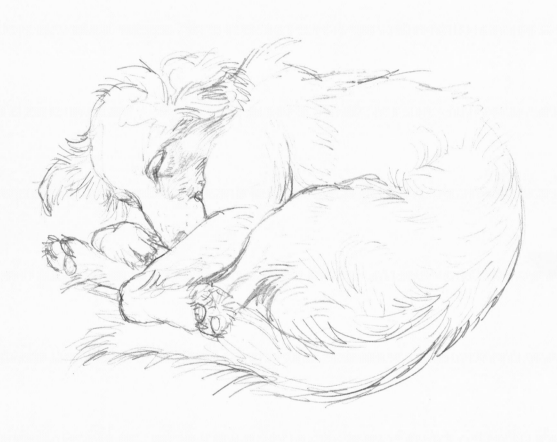

Animals in repose

The first demonstration on pages 22–3 is of a sleeping cat. The cat has a habit of adopting many unconventional positions in sleep, at first on her side, curled up, but after a time stretching, rolling over, and settling for the next period of slumber into a posture of uninhibited relaxation. Many pencil drawings were done in preparation and the drawings reproduced are about half the number done; several were sufficiently complete to serve as a basis for a finished picture; some of the incomplete ones were left unfinished because the cat moved; others were drawn as detailed notes to clarify the structure or position of feet, ears etc.

Of the complete figures, I chose for my picture one which shows the cat in an unexpected attitude.

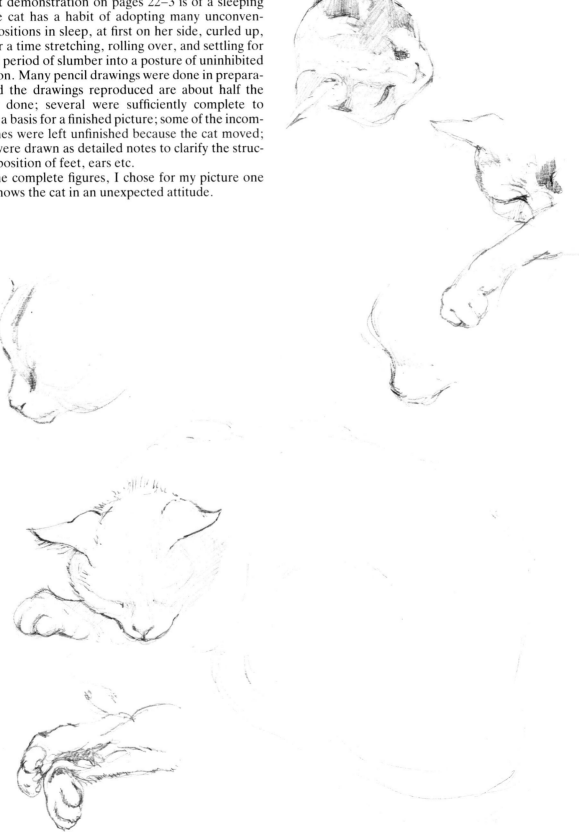

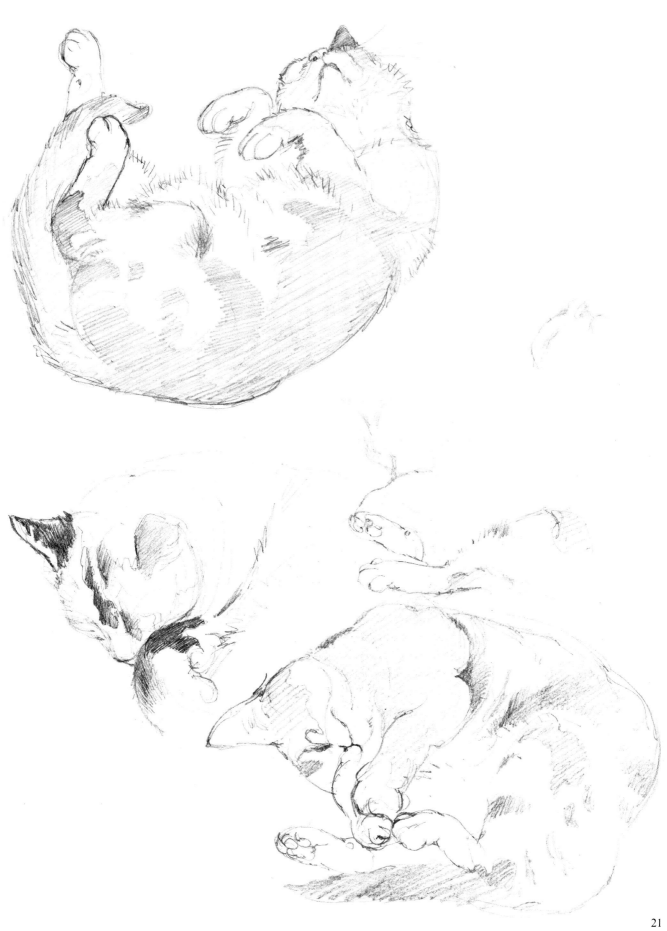

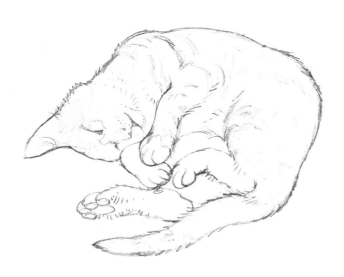

Stage 1

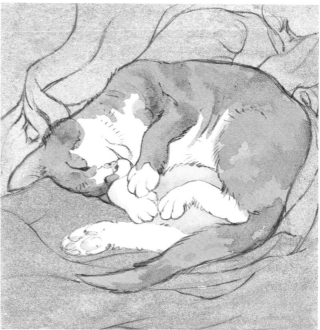

Stage 2

Sleeping cat: demonstration

Original size: 225mm sq./8¾in. sq.
Paper: Mould-made Fabriano 300gsm/140lb.

The first stage of producing any picture is, strictly speaking, that of looking at the subject and choosing which aspect of it to work on. This stage has been discussed on page 20, so we will call stage 1 of the demonstration that point at which the business begins of putting the chosen composition on paper.

Stage 1

Choose a suitable paper, and re-draw the cat carefully in the required size, the tortoiseshell markings lightly indicated, and the folds of the rumpled candlewick counterpane carefully drawn. This stage is very important, and must not be hurried. If possible, compare your drawings with the cat itself, as well as with your original sketch. It will not be in the same position, but its component parts will not have changed, and you will be able to check on such details as numbers of toes, and the relative position of ear, eyes and nose; turn your picture upside down and look at it in a mirror. Often this will reveal slight errors of drawing, and these must be rectified now – if you let them pass they will show up and haunt you later.

Stage 2

This is a simpler stage. I first go over the whole background with clean water, not quite up to the edges of the

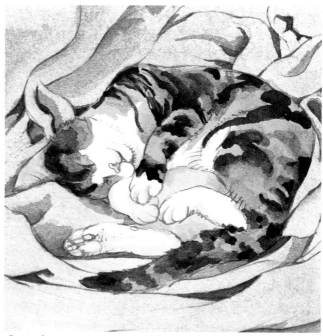

Stage 3

cat. A thin mixture of cobalt blue and Payne's grey is then washed quickly over the damp paper with a large brush, then with a fine brush the wet colour is carefully taken up to the edges of the cat.

When this is dry, the main colour of the cat (burnt sienna and yellow ochre) is put all over those parts of the cat which are not white, building up the blotches with stronger colour before it is dry. The toes, nose and ears are added with a thin mixture of permanent rose and cadmium red light.

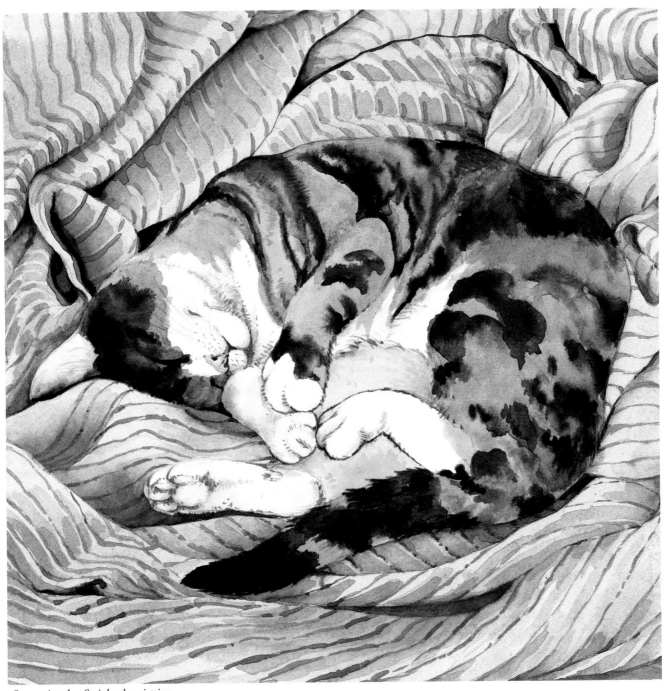

Stage 4 – the finished painting

Stage 3

A similar method is used to add the cat's black markings with a wash of lamp black. The colour must be floated on very delicately, so as not to disturb the colour beneath, in a thin wet wash, adding a stronger mixture of pigment and water as it dries, to give the range from solid black to mixed black and ginger stripes. A very weak wash of yellow ochre and black is used to model the white areas, and the folds in the cloth defined with a strong blue/grey mixture weakened where required with water.

Stage 4 – the finished painting

Apart from the addition of a few details of hair, whiskers, lips, nostrils, and variations of the colour of fur with patches of yellow or burnt sienna, the main work of this stage is the candlewick texture of the blue cloth. This takes a long time, but it justifies the effort by enriching the picture. The lines of blue-grey, dark or pale, according to their place on the folds, help to define their shapes, and form an interesting contrast to the irregular pattern of the cat's markings.

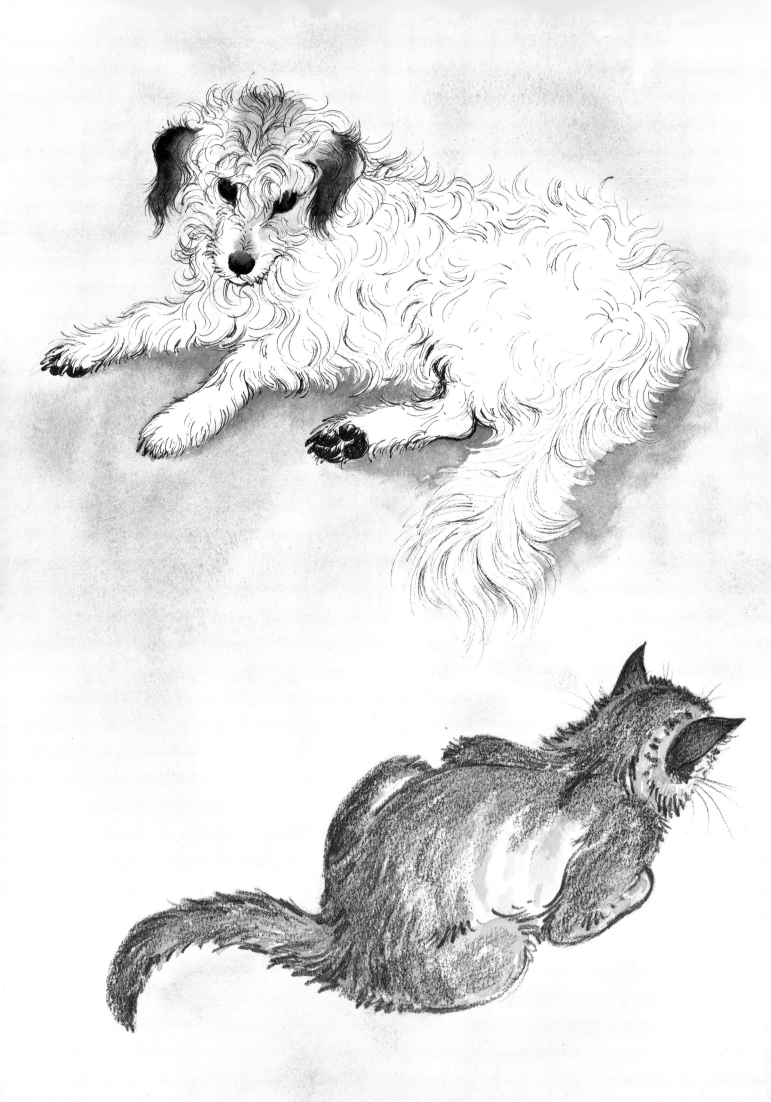

Capturing your subject

The drawings on these two pages are of animals not actually asleep, but in resting positions. There will always be some movement from animals in such postures, but unless your subject actually walks away, it is possible to continue drawing the body, and doing legs and head when they are in the right position. The best approach to subject is probably to draw the whole figure as quickly as is consistent with a careful look to sum up the elements of the pose, and then to continue, for as long as your model remains, to develop the drawing, correcting if necessary, and filling it out with more detail, and more thorough development of the forms.

The three pictures here are all made using different media, although in each watercolour is used to a greater or lesser extent. The white dog is a pen drawing with a small amount of watercolour – the pen line suits the subject, whose outstanding characteristic is the coat of longish disordered curls: the fine line indicates the shape of these without falsifying the light tone. The cat has more watercolour in its composition – in fact all the ginger part of its tortoiseshell pattern, the black part being carried out with a thick soft pencil, as is the main figure.

The other dog is painted almost entirely in watercolour, but soft white chalk has been used on the long plumy hair of its tail and ruff. This technique is a very useful mixture of media for depicting animals; so often the character rests on the convincing realisation of a rather diffuse but quite definite pale or white texture or pattern of fur over a much darker background. This is a method that can be used successfully for this purpose.

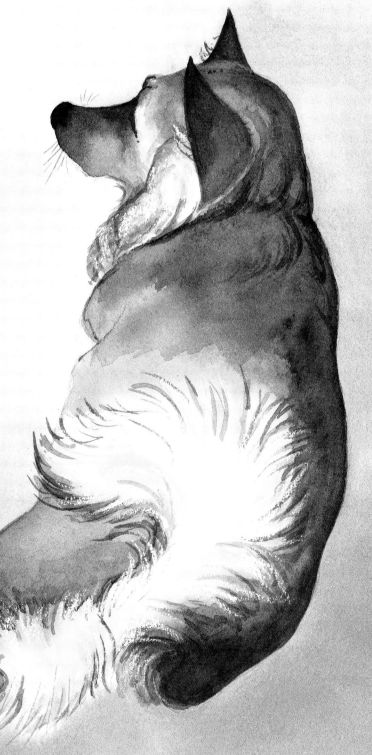

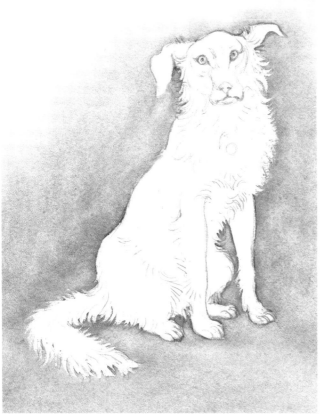

Stage 1

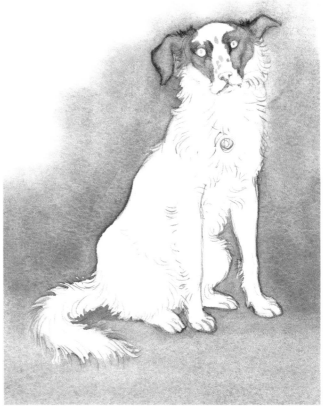

Stage 2

Sitting dog: demonstration

Original size: 290 × 222/11½ × 8¾in.
Paper: Russell Flint handmade 410gsm/200lb.

Stage 1

This lively young dog does not stay long in any one place; the pose was chosen from the usual preliminary sketches in varying degrees of completeness, and a pencil drawing was made on a rough hand-made paper.

The background is well wetted with clean water, up to about ¼in. from the edges of the animal. As she is mostly white, the background is used as a simple contrast, to define the figure. While the water soaks into the paper, I mix a plentiful supply of colour: manganese blue, phthalocyanine blue, and yellow ochre. I wet the paper again, then as quickly as possible apply the colour to the background and, with a smaller brush, take the colour up to the edges of the dog while the background is still wet, thus allowing the texture of the paper to give some variety of tone and colour in this background wash. The edge is softened in places with a clean wet brush, but these must be allowed to dry completely before any more work is done.

Stage 2

The colour for the dog's face-patches is mixed with yellow ochre and burnt sienna, washed on, and the tone built up with applications of more colour as it dries to model the form of the face and ears.

Stage 3 – the finished painting

The golden yellow eyes, brownish-grey nose, the collar and name-disc are added and, when they are dry, the nostrils, pupils and the edges of the eyelids and lips defined. The white parts of the dog are now given a little more modelling with a pale mixture of yellow ochre and black. In this picture the pencil drawing plays an important part, being used to indicate the hair and details of feet and muzzle.

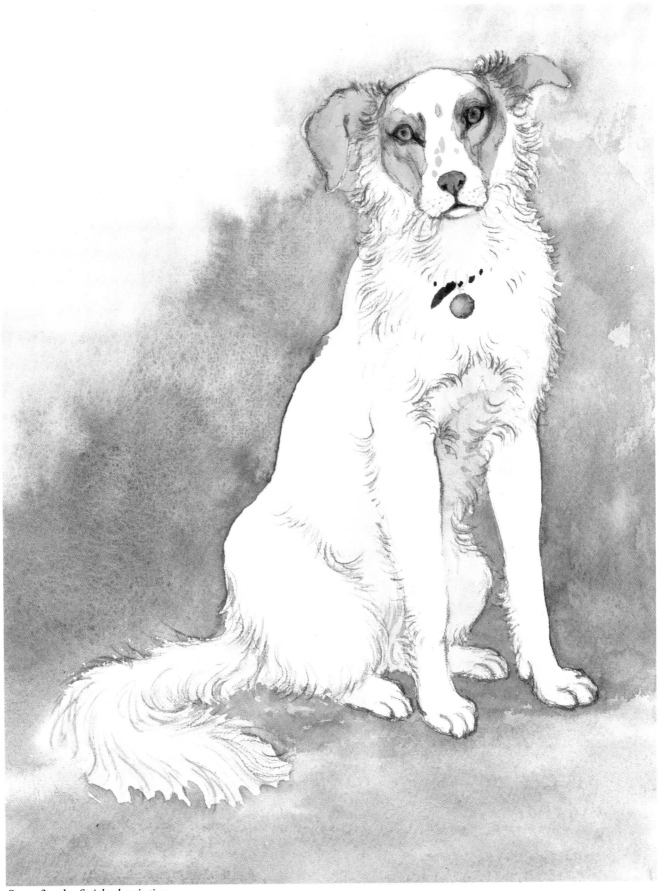

Stage 3 – the finished painting

Painting animals in watercolour

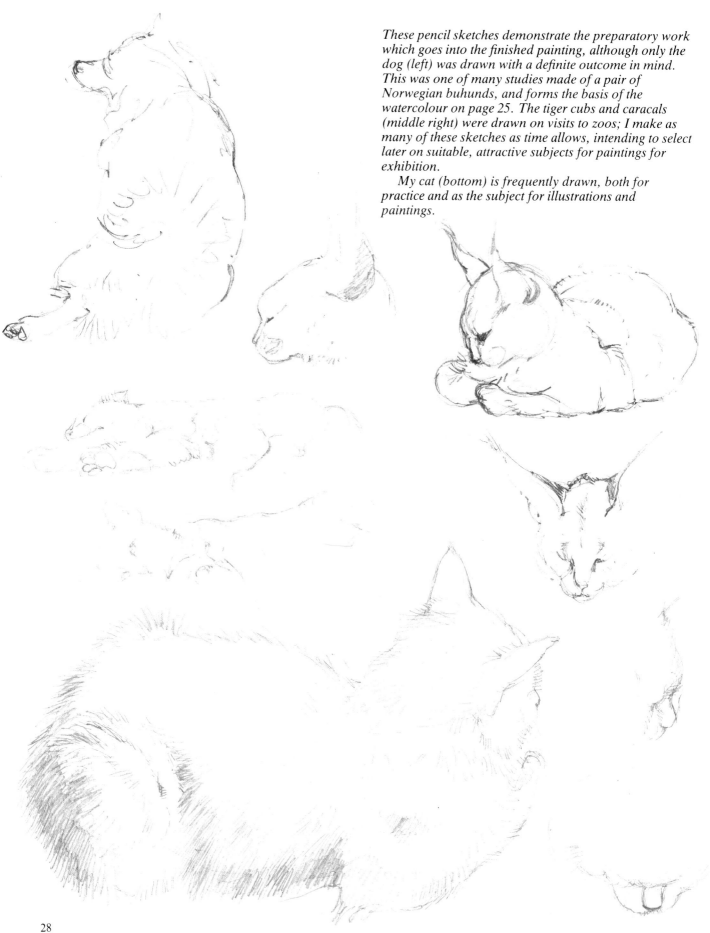

These pencil sketches demonstrate the preparatory work which goes into the finished painting, although only the dog (left) was drawn with a definite outcome in mind. This was one of many studies made of a pair of Norwegian buhunds, and forms the basis of the watercolour on page 25. The tiger cubs and caracals (middle right) were drawn on visits to zoos; I make as many of these sketches as time allows, intending to select later on suitable, attractive subjects for paintings for exhibition.

My cat (bottom) is frequently drawn, both for practice and as the subject for illustrations and paintings.

ANIMALS
IN MOVEMENT

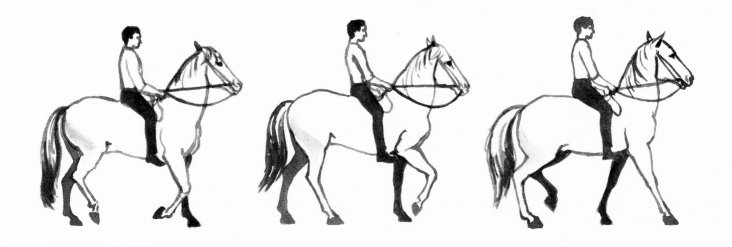

Animals in movement

When animals move, the difficulties of drawing them obviously increase enormously. Also, the faster the movement is, the greater is the difficulty of seeing, let alone drawing, the mechanics of the motion. There are several ways in which enlightenment can be sought.

It is possible to perceive certain positions or postures that an animal assumes in the course of moving, which it seems to hold for rather longer than others. These are the stages in the whole sequence of positions that will best portray the action, and are the right ones to pick for your drawing. The great difficulty however, lies in seeing for certain the relationship to each other of all parts of the animal at a given moment in the course of the action.

The sequence of drawings below, and on page 29, are based on two of a great volume of sequences of photographs of moving animals and humans, the product of the remarkable Eadweard Muybridge (born Edward Muggeridge) who, in the latter part of the nineteenth century, starting in May 1872, devised a means of photographing moving animals at regular, minute intervals providing, by this means, an answer to questions that had stumped experts at least since (according to Plato) the time of the ancient Egyptians. The drawings on page 29 are based on photographs selected from one of Muybridge's sequences of a walking horse, and those on this page and the next on his photographs illustrating the canter. There are many other gaits and animals shown in his work – cattle, deer, pigs, raccoons, cockatoos, ostriches, pigeons, dogs and cats, as well as horses. The same information is now supplied by cinematograph film and video, and these, particularly in showing slow motion, are extremely useful to the artist.

Constant drawing of moving animals, that is, recording positions of legs, neck and tail, rather than attempting any comprehensive representation of form, will not only supply information but develop one's ability to perceive actions. Drawings done at this speed must be used only in conjunction with others done at greater leisure or with a study of the animal, referring back to your action sketches. Still photographs of the same species or breed can also be used, so long as one refrains from copying a photo but uses the information it supplies to augment that obtained from your drawings.

The other valuable aid to understanding the processes of movement is some acquaintance with the anatomy of the animal, not necessarily in great detail, but sufficient to help one realise what underlies its outward appearance; which parts of it are fixed, which parts move, and in how many directions; which bits can be stretched and which cannot. This subject is dealt with on pages 96–7, but from the drawings it can be seen that the movement of the fore and rear pairs of legs arises in different ways; the hind legs pivot from a point about half-way down the body, where the thigh-bone articulates with the pelvis; the forelegs' action arises from the top of the body, the shoulder-blades moving with the foreleg bones, and pivoting from the level of the backbone. This is shown in some drawings, likewise on pages 96–7, which are based on more of Muybridge's photographs, with lines superimposed to show the positions of the bones of the legs.

While a deep study of anatomy is not necessary, reference to the workings of skeleton and muscles can so illuminate a puzzling question in drawing an animal that there is much to be said for getting into the habit of referring to the skeleton whenever you find a form difficult to draw. At times it is hard to work out just why a subject is as it is, but this is so clarified by going a little deeper into the matter that the difficulty lessens and disappears. Many museums have at least some animal skeletons.

After some familiarity with the skeleton has been achieved, it can be very useful to augment this by finding out in a practical way how the skeleton is moved by the actions of a living animal. In the course of stroking and fondling a reasonably even-tempered cat or dog, one can glean a lot of useful information about the positions of bones, the relative lengths of different parts of the skeleton, and the range of movement of the various joints. Gently and slowly moving the legs about can be most illuminating; it is important to study this aspect of an animal's appearance, as well as the static forms.

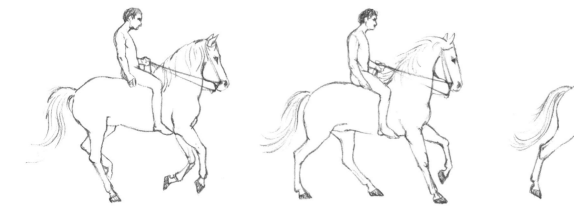

The drawings on this page all represent endeavours to capture movement in varying degrees; gentle, slight motion of tails and heads in the cow and calf sketch (one of preparatory studies for the demonstration on pages 118 and 119); rapid turns, bucking and galloping by the gnus (left). As these were drawn from television, with its constant changes of viewpoint, I had to work even faster than when drawing directly from the living animals.

The raccoon's steady prowling round and round his small enclosure meant that I saw the same view of him at regular intervals, at least until he changed his route. The common toad might seem to present less difficulty in this respect, but he can put on quite a turn of speed.

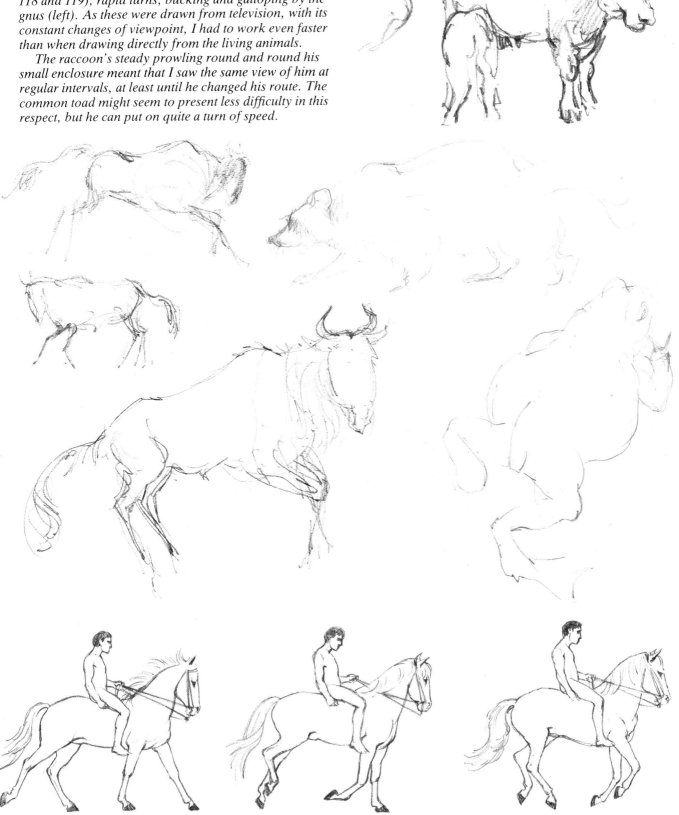

Run, rabbit

The positions of the rabbit at the bottom of this page, three stages of a fast run, show what a considerable distance is covered by each stride, as both pairs of legs stretch out horizontally; the hind feet overtake the front feet as they touch the ground, and the powerful hind legs give another strong push which propels the animal far forward. The feet work very nearly as separate pairs, fore and rear, but they are very slightly out of synchronisation with each other, though so little that to the unaided vision it looks as though each pair of feet is moving together.

Other animals move their legs almost simultaneously in pairs, but in a different arrangement – both left legs then both right legs together – these tend to be large, heavy animals such as bears and elephants, and also old cats and dogs.

When attempting to draw moving animals it is helpful to spend a considerable time simply watching, as there is no doubt that familiarity with the subject makes drawing it correctly both easier and quicker. In spite of the near impossibility of accurately fixing the sequence of limb movements of a fast-moving animal by the eye only, nevertheless as you watch it becomes clear that certain positions are in a way characteristic of a particular action, and convey it most clearly; perhaps this is because these positions are held just a little longer, but whatever the reason it is so. Studying the photographs of, for instance, all the horses running together in a race, will show that the attitudes of some of the horses look right and convey swift and energetic movement, while a few will look rather odd, almost awkward, though obviously they, just as much as the others, are moving their legs in the correct order.

It cannot be over-emphasized that in drawing a moving animal from life, even the most slight and incomplete drawings are of value, and well worth keeping; any unfinished detail may prove to be the one that provides the exact piece of information you need, perhaps long afterwards, when used in conjunction with other drawings done on different occasions. If all your drawings of a particular animal, or kind of animal, are kept together and referred to when you embark on a painting, so that you have all the data at your disposal, you are giving yourself the best chance of producing a good sound piece of work.

A moving animal seems almost to change its shape as it moves, not merely its position. A neck which, in repose, seems almost non-existent can extend in a way that suggests that its structure is like that of a telescope; in fact, the truth is more likely to be that the skeleton of the neck is flexed, almost folded into a double curve, within its wall of muscles, and hidden in its loose and elastic covering of furry skin, so that when its owner wishes to strike forward suddenly, or to see over an obstruction, the whole extends itself very fast and to a surprising length. Seals and cats are particularly gifted in this respect. Both seem able at will to vary their shape from a very long and slender one to something approaching the spherical. A cat sitting out of doors on a cold day will be very little longer than it is wide, its head will be settled comfortably well into its shoulders, legs tucked under its body, and tail wrapped round to keep out the draught. The same cat, reaching up to a table-top or a door-handle, will have changed those proportions completely, and be apparently twice its former length and half its width.

The running rabbit shows some of the same kind of change of shape; although the neck is not extended, the body and legs alternate between long and narrow, and bunched up and compact.

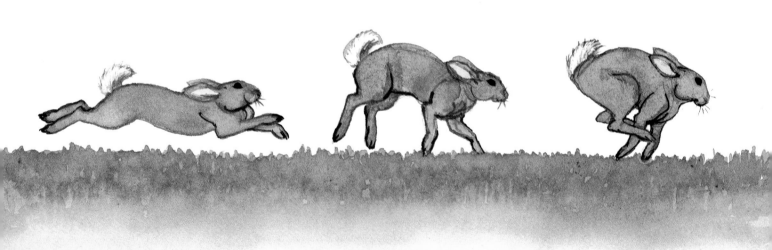

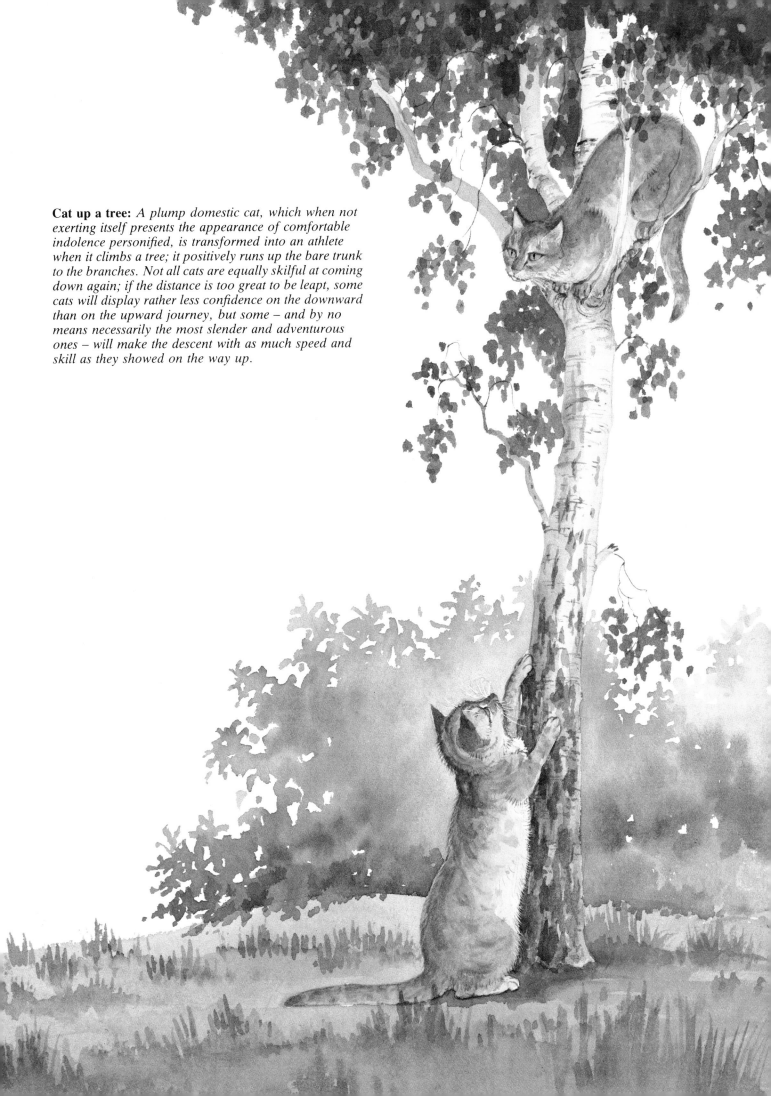

Cat up a tree: *A plump domestic cat, which when not exerting itself presents the appearance of comfortable indolence personified, is transformed into an athlete when it climbs a tree; it positively runs up the bare trunk to the branches. Not all cats are equally skilful at coming down again; if the distance is too great to be leapt, some cats will display rather less confidence on the downward than on the upward journey, but some – and by no means necessarily the most slender and adventurous ones – will make the descent with as much speed and skill as they showed on the way up.*

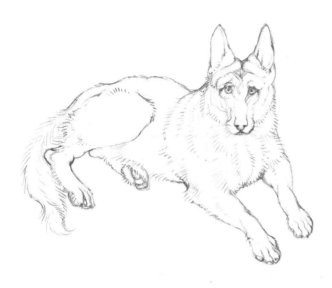

Stage 1

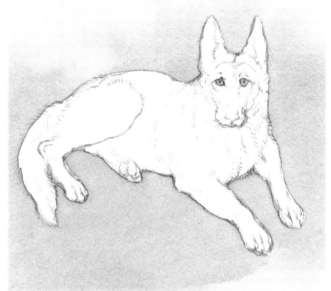

Stage 2

Alsatian puppy: demonstration

Original size: 225mm sq./9in. sq.
Paper: Mould-made Whatman 180gsm/90lb.

The young Alsatian, past the stage of infancy but still a puppy in behaviour at about six months of age, does not stay still for long except when asleep. Many quick drawings were made, and several were combined to supply the basis of the chosen pose; one drawing showed the entire body and legs, so that nothing was invented. The position of the head was taken from another drawing in which the body was incomplete.

Stage 1

The final drawing is done from life, working over a basic re-drawing of the first sketches. It is not necessary to see the dog in an identical position – that was obtained at the first sitting, and now only needs to be developed into a firm pencil study by means of constant reference to the animal.

Stage 2

The eyes are given their base-colour of mixed burnt sienna and yellow; the background is wetted all over; a mixture of pthalocyanine blue, cadmium yellow light, and Payne's grey gives the desired greyish green, and is used to build up a preliminary tone around the form of the dog, although the final tone will be adjusted later.

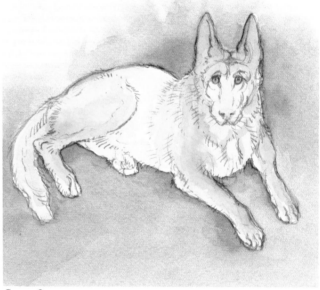

Stage 3

Stage 3

When the background colour is absolutely dry, a ground-tone of mixed yellow ochre and burnt sienna is washed over the dog, varying from very pale to a warm brown on the head and other parts, where extra burnt sienna is added to the still damp wash. The background tone is built up with the grey-green, with extra Payne's grey added to the mixture.

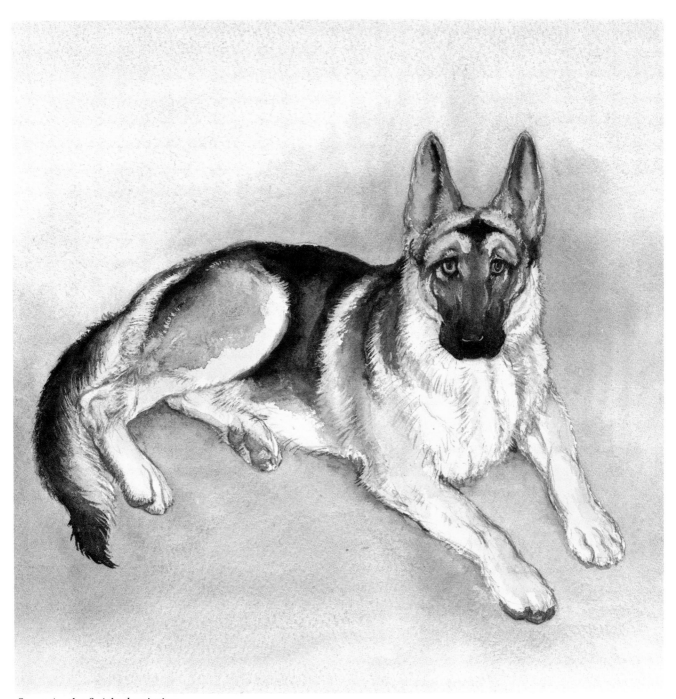

Stage 4 – the finished painting

Stage 4 – the finished painting

A wash of lamp black, varying from thick to very thin, is put over all those parts of the dog where the coat is black or where black hairs overlie the brown; some ultramarine on the flank gives the light reflected by the glossy black hair. A thin black wash is put on the pads, and used for details of dark hairs; light hairs are defined with opaque yellowish white. Details on eyes and muzzle are defined in black, and highlights touched in with opaque white and grey. The final tone of the background can be built up a little more if wished.

Animals in motion

While it is natural to think of an animal in motion as one which is walking, running, leaping, climbing or in some way proceeding from one place to another, there are many other kinds of movement which can provide interest in a picture. A few are shown here, portrayed in some different ways:

The little dog scratching its ear is drawn with an extra thick soft pencil; the cat lapping milk is painted with a wet black wash on wet paper, with a few details added once the wash is dry – eyes, tongue, ears and a few hairs, and the blue saucer.

The cat washing is also done with a single wash, but with the edges dry, not the soft diffused edge one gets on a wet ground. Much more detail was added over the wash after it dried; stripes, details of feet, ears, and more hairs, including the hair growth pattern on the back of its neck.

The fourth figure, the sleeping cat, is drawn with a fine brush, and defines the hair to a still greater extent. A slight wash of tone is added to this detailed brush drawing, which was then completed with the addition of pink ears, nose, eyelids, mouth and toes.

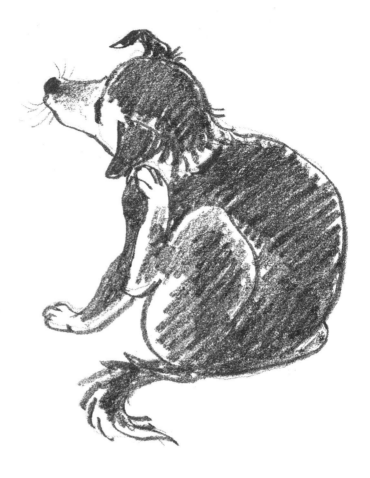

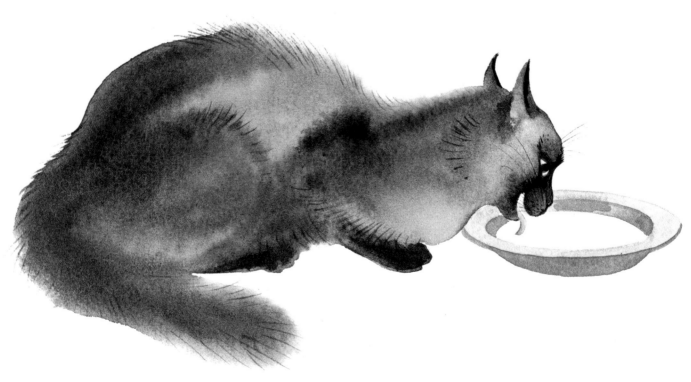

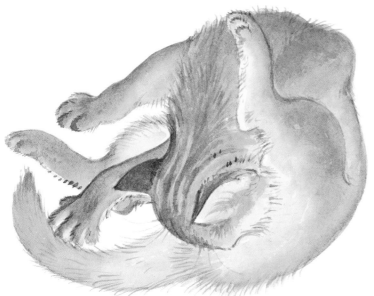

Leaping cat: demonstration *(pages 38–9)*

Original size: 290 × 222/11½ × 8¾in.
Paper: Saunders 180gsm/90lb.

In order to maintain the impression of fairly rapid movement in the picture of a cat leaping down from a height, I decided to use a generally fluid, loose treatment. The picture is almost entirely in closely related colours in the yellow to red sector, while a contrasting note is supplied by the green eyes and black pupils.

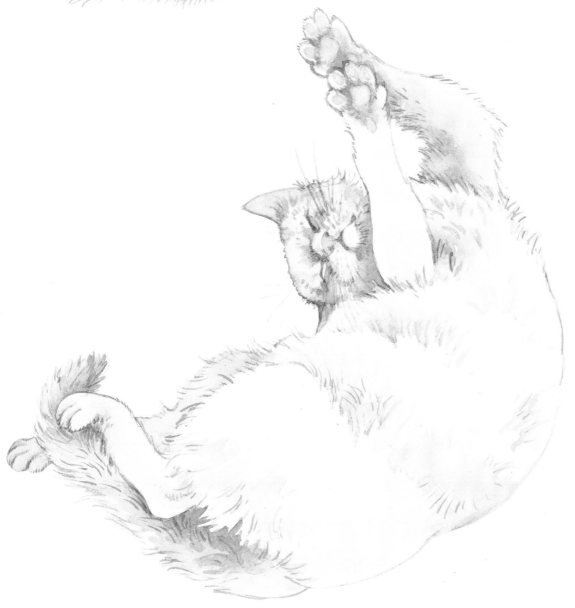

Painting animals in watercolour

Stage 1

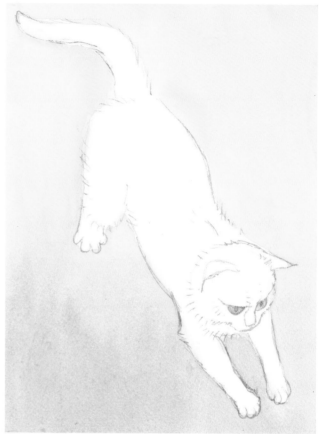

Stage 2

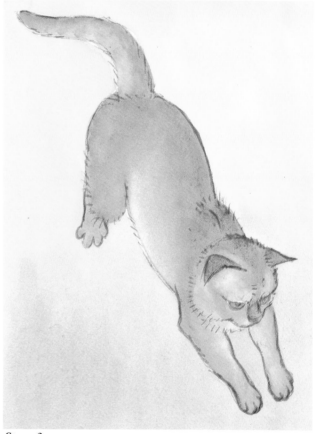

Stage 3

Stage 1

The cat is drawn as it nears the ground – the front paws in position for landing, the hind feet coming forward and down ready to hit the ground immediately afterwards, the toes spread in preparation. The eyes are put in with pale green.

Stage 2

A wash is put over the entire background, a pale warm yellow at the top, graduating to a warm brown at the bottom. A very small amount of violet is added at the bottom left corner so that the background hues are not identical with those of the cat's fur.

Stage 3

The whole cat's body is washed over with diluted burnt sienna, ranging from dark on the back and face to nearly white on the underside of the animal's left foreleg.

Stage 4 – the finished painting

The cat's markings are added with a thicker burnt sienna wash, softened at the edges. A darker colour is used to delineate ears, hairs, fur, nose and forms round the eyes, and black for the pupils.

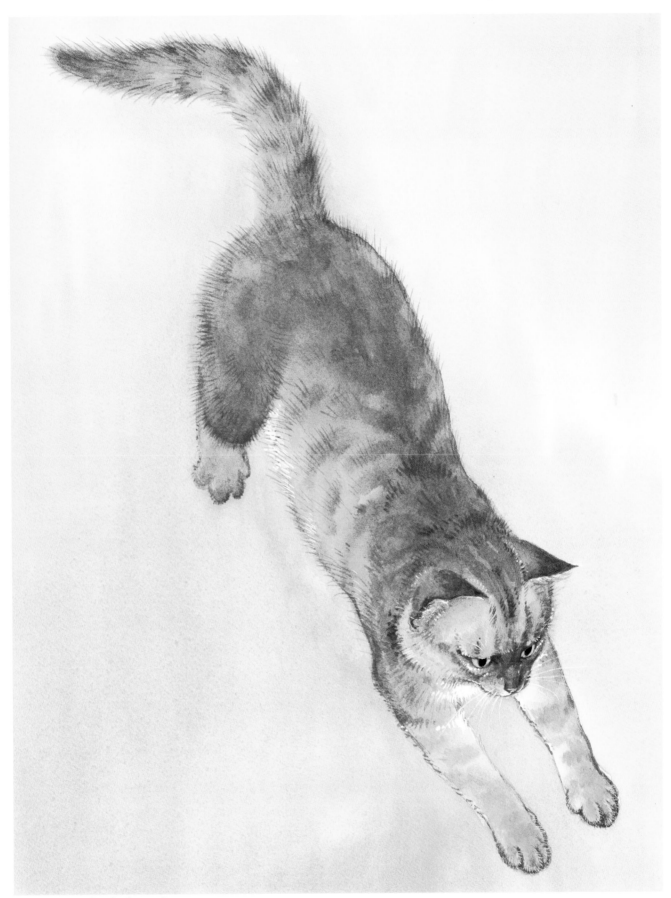

Stage 4 – the finished painting

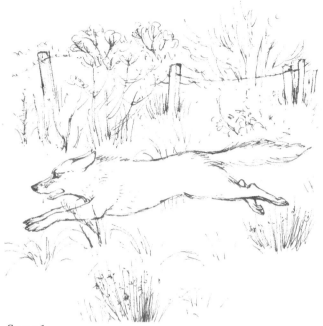

Stage 1

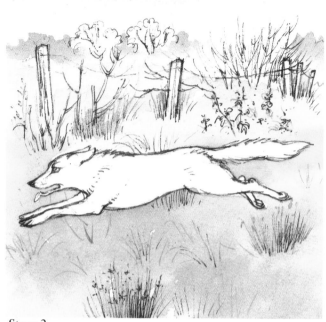

Stage 2

Fox: demonstration

Original size: 225mm sq./9in. sq.
Paper: Mould-made Whatman 180gsm/90lb.

Stage 1

The figure of the fox is carefully drawn, using many studies from life and from filmed wild animals, details and measurements being checked by reference to photographs and to measured drawings made from dead specimens. This is then developed into a pen drawing, with the essentials completed but the finishing to be done later.

Stage 2

Pale washes are applied: cobalt blue for the sky; blue-green on the field; yellow ochre and a variety of greens in the foreground, some bright and yellowish, some with more blue.

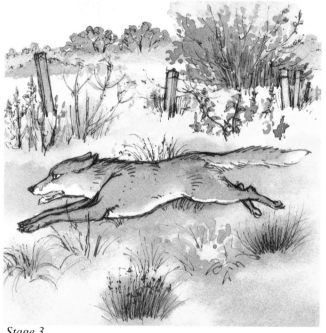

Stage 3

Stage 3

This process is taken further – a blue/grey/green for the bush on the right of the picture, yellow-olive for the oak trees in the background and a brighter green for the other distant trees. A mixture of green, yellow and brown is used for the fence-posts, burnt sienna for the sorrel, yellow ochre for the dried stalks of the cow parsley; and dots of yellow for the flowers, dark green for the nettles, and a stronger bluer green for the clumps of reeds. A basic wash of burnt sienna is then put over the figure of the fox.

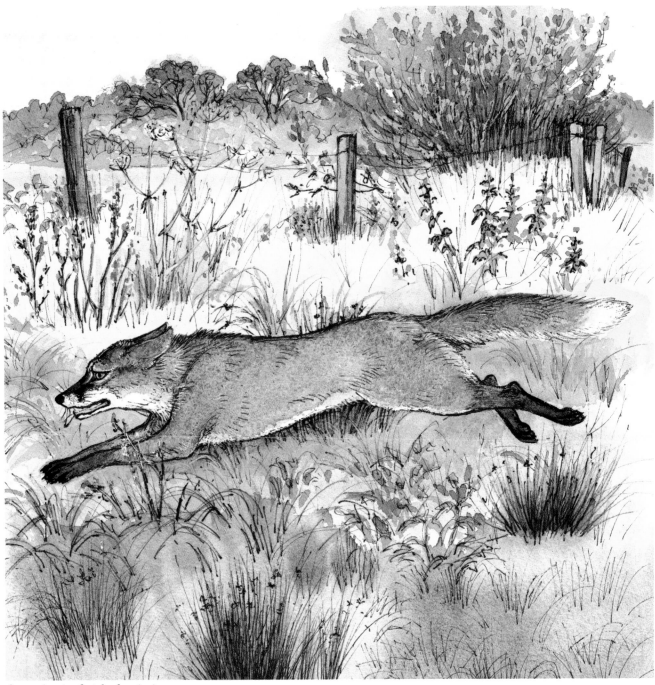

Stage 4 – the finished painting

Stage 4 – the finished painting

The figure of the fox is now completed with a black wash of varied strength: intense on feet and muzzle; a thin wash on the body and tail. The texture of the paper gives a happy effect to this combination of two separate washes.

A great deal of detail is added to the background, both in watercolour (notably the bright yellow-green leaves around the left-hand fence-post and foliage) and in pen, with details of branches, leaves, grass, reeds, posts and wire. The same is done for the fox, with whitish hairs on the tail, head, neck, chest and rump, and a lot more pen drawing of details of hairs, toes, claws, eye and whiskers.

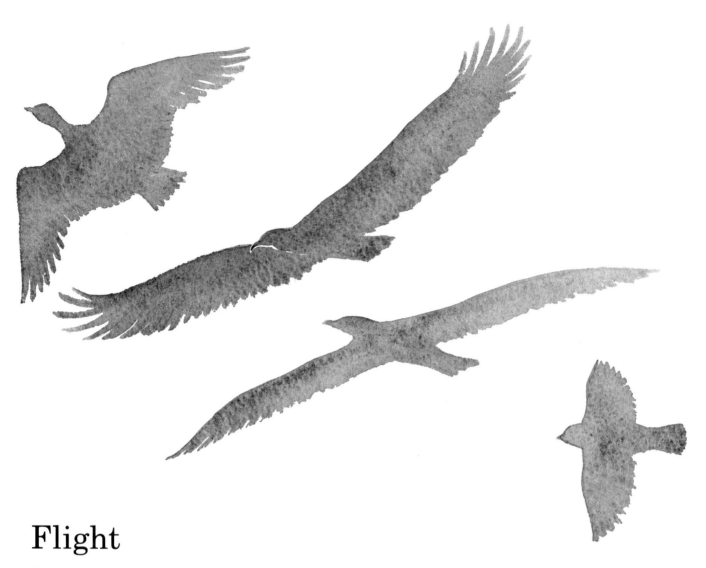

Flight

The important topic of flight, and how birds achieve it, can be dealt with here in only the most general terms. Considering the size of most birds, and the fact that in many cases their fuel comes in very small units – such as insects, seeds, caterpillars, or berries – their performance in flying at all seems almost incredible. Migratory flights of many hundreds of miles represent quite extraordinary activity for a creature whose weight is often only a matter of ounces.

Even to lift so small and light a body as a song-bird's, and to move two such relatively large appendages as wings, requires muscles which, in relation to the bird's size, are massive and powerful. This in turn means that a large, steady frame must be provided for these muscles to arise from; that proportionately large lungs are necessary to sustain the considerable effort of flying; and that this effort must be used to its best effect by so streamlining the head and body that it goes through the air without providing any more resistance than is necessary. It is these considerations which govern the typical bird shape: more or less oval, with no sudden protuberances, and legs that are usually drawn up like a retractable undercarriage, except for

the long legs of storks, flamingoes and such birds, which trail behind them.

When drawing, the same considerations apply to flying birds as to galloping horses – observe as much as possible, and study photographs to confirm and expand your observations. At least when birds glide, as do many of the most impressive long-distance fliers, it is possible to see what they are doing as they soar and swoop.

The shape of a bird's wings is governed by its way of life: vultures, eagles, and albatrosses, which fly vast distances or soar to great heights, and remain airborne for long periods, have long wings with strong primary feathers to control their soaring and gliding, and to make the most of wind and rising air.

Geese, swans, and other heavy large-bodied birds, which also fly great distances in regular migrations, have broad wings both to lift their bulk (with a great deal of noise) and keep them flying strongly to and from arctic and temperate zones and back again.

Small birds which live among bushes and trees have rather short wings and so can fly safely between the branches.

DOGS

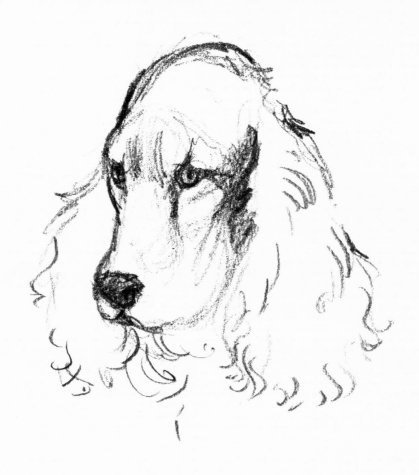

Dogs

Although the domestic dog is a single species, the range of dogs' sizes, shapes and coats is extraordinary. It shows what can be achieved by interfering with the course of nature and causing animals to breed together in order to intensify 'particular characteristics – what might be termed 'unnatural selection'. Theoretically any dog will breed with any other; in practice of course, enormously exaggerated discrepancies in size can prevent such inter-breeding from being achieved successfully. There is no doubt in the mind of a dog, however, about his close relationship with a bitch of another breed.

The results of 'accidental' crosses are as good dogs as their artificially engineered relations, and often as hand-some; indeed one may feel that in this respect they are superior to some of the dog breeders' flights of fancy.

Dogs who are incapable of breathing normally, like bulldogs; whose backs cannot support their own weight, like dachshunds; whose eyes are easily dislocated (pekingese), or who are too small to give birth safely by normal means (the smaller chihuahuas), are not the result of matings arranged by the dogs themselves but of those masterminded by man.

The repeated random matings of non-pedigree dogs, on the other hand, tend to produce eventually quite a respectable looking animal, with no exaggerated charac-teristics; not so very different from a jackal, which is a small wolf.

The drawings on this page show some of the variations of the build, proportions and coat of the products of dog-breeding.

The top one, an elkhound, is the closest to the wolf-like animal from which all domestic dogs are most probably descended.

Next, a greyhound – one of the oldest of breeds, with long legs and long jaws.

The dachshund is the victim of breeding that has nearly got rid of its legs; this breed suffers greatly from slipped discs.

The King Charles spaniel has an abnormally short nose, and an abnormally long and wavy coat.

The fox terrier shows no extraordinary distortions. Although it was born with a normal tail, this was cut off.

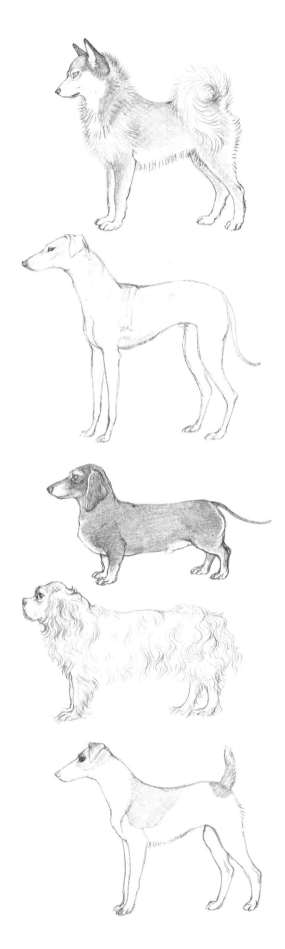

Anatomy and physique

The drawings on this page show some of what underlies the outward appearance of some dogs, and demonstrates the extent to which the skeleton has had its proportions altered with selective breeding. The two shown here started from the same point, and whereas the top one is almost the same as its early forebears, considerable modifications have been made to the skeleton of the other. The short legs mean that the upper leg bones consist of little more than the two ends, the middle part having been reduced almost to nothing. Nevertheless the relationship between the two is still very clear.

These alterations to the dog's physique were begun with a purpose in mind, of course, and most breeds have a perfectly sensible build and pleasing appearance; it is when these breeds are no longer bred for the original purpose, or when the standards are set only for competing in shows, that the desired physical characteristics become extreme, and appearance is of more importance than performance. If modern specimens of a particular breed are compared with photographs of dogs of that breed of a century or more ago, considerable differences are seen – short legs are shorter, pushed back noses have been pushed back almost in line with the eyes, long coats have become a floor-length curtain of hair. Where the dog has continued to be used for its purpose, there has been a divergence between the working and show types, as with collies. Working collies have continued without much change this century; the present-day Rough collies have a longer nose and longer silkier fur, though they still retain their shepherding instinct and individuals occasionally work with sheep alongside their more workaday relations.

The lower drawings show the differences between a normal dog's skull and the greatly distorted one of a bulldog. Here again, the change began so that the dog could grip a lump of the bull with its teeth without its nostrils being stopped up. At the beginning of the century, the nostrils were about half-way between the front teeth and the eyes; now when very few bulldogs need to have their noses anywhere but in the front of their faces, they are about as far back as they will go, and bulldogs have to snuffle and gasp for breath.

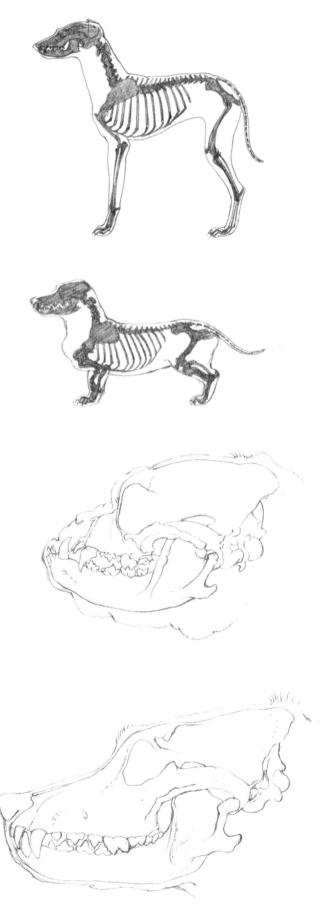

Dog, walking: demonstration

Original size: 185 × 375mm/7¼ × 15in.
Paper: Saunders 180gsm/90lb.

The gait of a dog walking on its own is quite different from that of a dog on a lead. The golden labrador in this picture ambles along sampling the interesting scents left by previous travellers.

Stage 1

As always, the drawing is of prime importance; it is not essential to include a lot of detail as long as you have detailed studies to work from, or the living animal. It is vital that what you draw is in the right place.

Stage 2

The background is left vague, simple washes of colour to suggest a rough path and verdure. These are applied to previously wetted paper in bands of yellow-green, with darker bluer green above, and greyish brown below.

Stage 3

When this is thoroughly dry a light wash of yellow ochre is put all over the dog – much paler on the inside of the far hind leg, and on the lower parts of the face and neck; deepened and warmed up with added burnt sienna on the crown, ear, neck, shoulders, rump and tail.

Stage 4 – the finished painting

All the sharp detail is added now; a black wash, with some burnt sienna in it, is used to model the structure of the face, mouth, eye and nose, building up with a less watery mixture, finally at almost full strength, to give the head considerable prominence. Further washes of warm brown are used on the ear, neck, shoulders and tail, where deeper coloured hair overlies the pale coat. Fine brush marks indicate the lie of the hair, and point up the details of ear, eye, and paws.

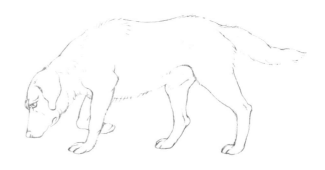

Stage 1

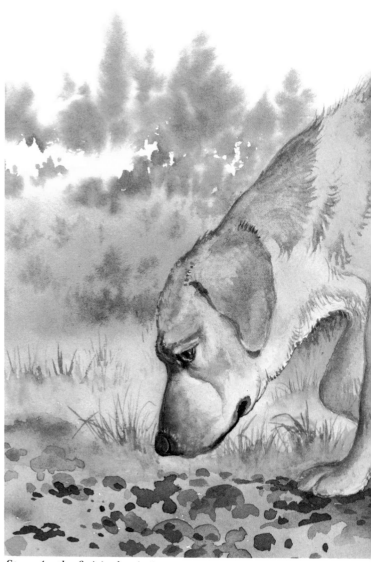

Stage 4 – the finished painting

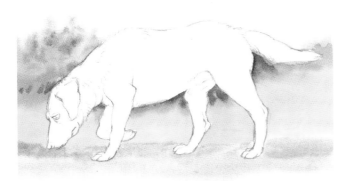

Stage 2

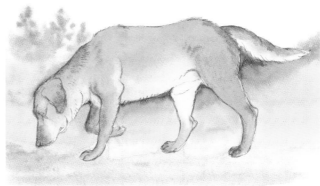

Stage 3

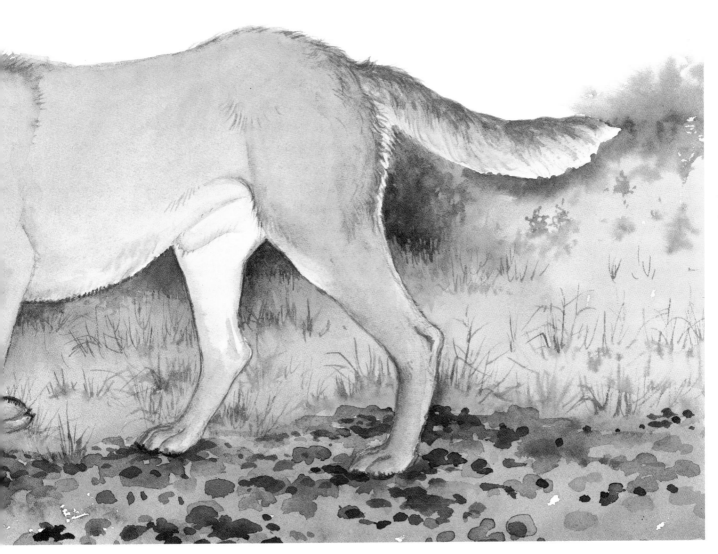

The Spitz group

These dogs are the nearest in appearance to wolves, not necessarily in size, as they range from the Eskimo dogs, which really are like wolves and which in fact have been known to interbreed with them, to the toy pomeranian. The characteristics of the group include upright pointed ears, tightly curled tails, pointed noses, and a thick springy coat.

The breed illustrated is a samoyed, and others of the group are elkhounds, chows, keeshonds and buhunds. The purposes for which these breeds were used are many – huskies for hauling, chows for food, elkhounds for hunting, pomeranians as lapdogs, spitzes for watchdogs as well as for hunting, buhunds for cattle herding, keeshonds for keeping on barges (presumably as watchdogs).

The samoyed picture is almost in monochrome, the only patch of colour is the pink tongue. Apart from the eyes, nose and mouth, the drawing consists mostly of hair – the coat is very dense and weather-resistant.

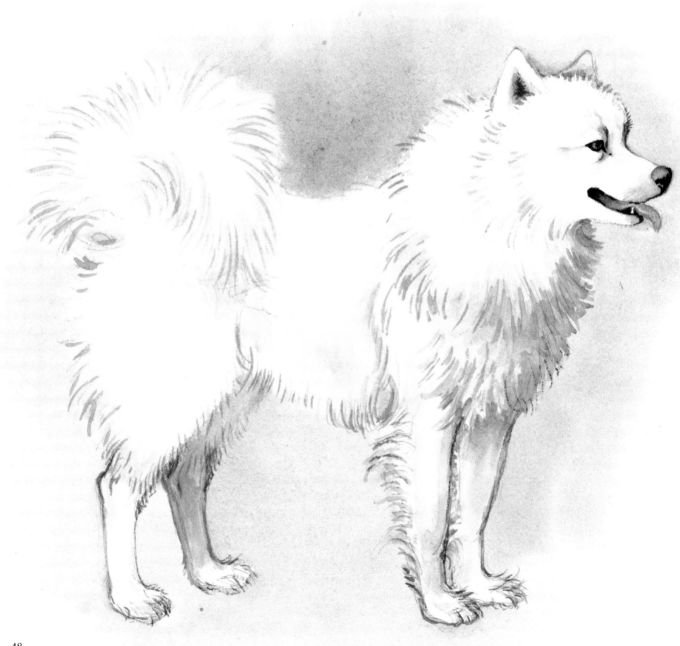

Spaniels

The spaniels and their related breeds have been bred mainly for retrieving, and are capable of carrying things in their mouths without inflicting damage; they also tend to plunge into water whenever the opportunity arises. There are many breeds of spaniel – the cockers, British and American, springer, clumber and water-spaniels; King Charles spaniels and papillons, and many others; the setters are in effect tall spaniels; retrievers and labradors may be regarded as related breeds.

They have silky, often wavy or curly coats, long soft ears, rather domed heads and soft baggy mouths. The drawings are studies of various spaniels; the colour illustration is of an English cocker spaniel; here again, much of the work in the picture consists of putting in the hair, which is much softer and smoother than the samoyed's, and wavy.

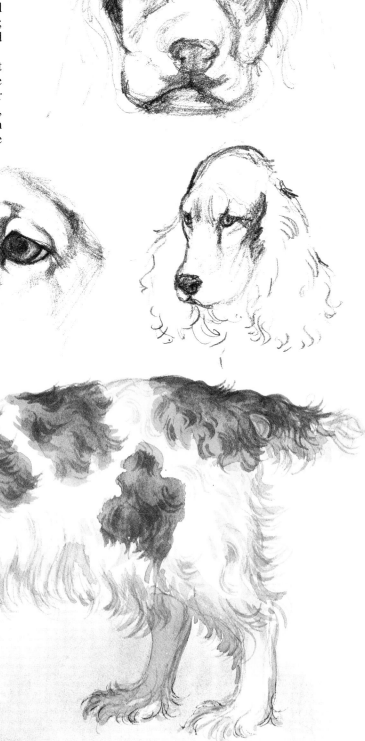

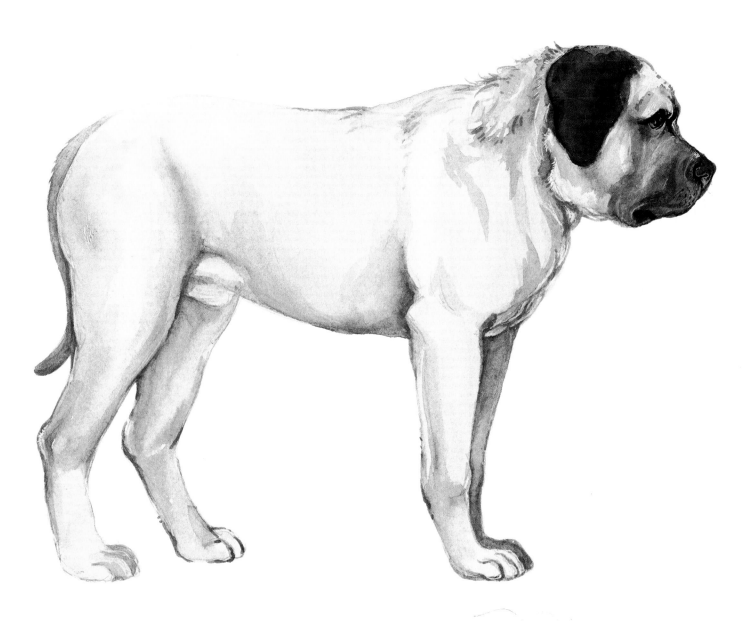

Mastiffs

Mastiffs are one of the oldest breeds of dog – a dog very similar to our present-day mastiff is shown in Assyrian reliefs. Most large, heavily-built dogs can be classified as varieties of mastiff: St Bernards, Pyrenean and Bernese mountain dogs, Great Danes, and Newfoundlands; bull mastiffs, bulldogs and boxers might also be included in this group.

The mastiff in the picture, unlike the previous two animals, is short-coated, so that its powerful heavy build is clearly seen; the skin on its head is looser and hangs heavily round its lower jaw, and above its eyes. The picture required careful drawing, but the watercolour treatment is straightforward and direct, with simple washes over the drawing, and a little reinforcement of details with a fine brush.

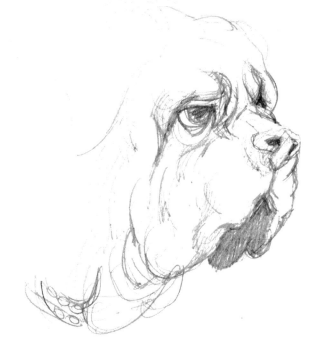

Terriers

The terriers form a very large group, varied in build and ranging in size from Airedales (not often seen nowadays, though quite common in the inter-war period) as big as retrievers, down to Yorkshire terriers, minute but well able to speak up for themselves. By definition terriers were bred for digging out unfortunate animals which had taken refuge underground. They come in almost any colour: black and tan, as in Airedales, Manchester, and Welsh terriers; black, as are Scottish terriers; blue-grey (Kerry Blues); white (West Highland terrier); brindle (Cairns); red-brown (Border terrier); yellow (Irish); or white with patches of tan, black or brindle, as in fox terriers and Jack Russells. Legs vary from long, as in Airedales, to almost none, as in Sealyhams.

The picture is of a wire-haired fox terrier – much the same animal as the smooth fox terrier on page 44 but with a wiry springy weather-proof coat. Comparison between the two pictures illustrates how, when drawing a long-coated dog, one must remain aware that what lies under the hair is an animal with muscles, bones and tendons.

Although at a cursory glance such an animal may look shapeless, and the arrangement of hair disordered, the position of each lock of hair is determined by its place on the solid dog beneath. Thorough study of the animal reveals this, and careful drawing will show both the nature of the coat and the form of the dog inside it.

Old English sheepdog: demonstration (*pages 52–3*)

Original size: 290 × 222mm/11½ × 8¾in.
Paper: Saunders 300gsm/140lb.

The shaggy coat and general build of this dog seem to make it a suitable subject for a very free, quick treatment. Inside the long thick coat is a large normally shaped dog, but the waving locks of hair are what fill the view.

Stage 1

First draw the figure of the dog, on an absorbent medium-rough paper. The grey parts of the dog – ear, back, and haunch – are then given a freely brushed wash of slightly bluish grey.

The whole shape of the dog is then outlined with curly brush strokes of masking fluid; this process is continued over all those parts of the dog which I want to keep white or very pale.

Stage 2

A very pale, yellow-grey is used on the parts which, though in light, need a little tone to show the individual

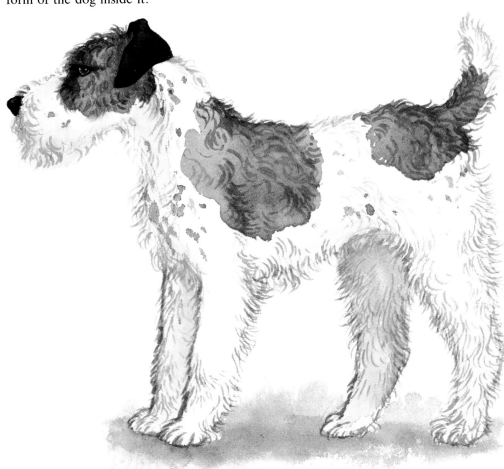

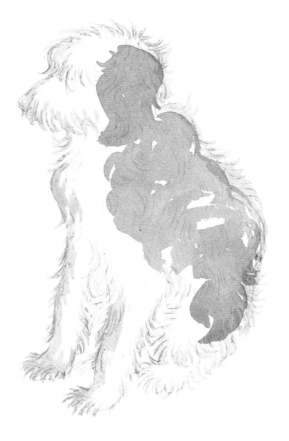

Stage 1

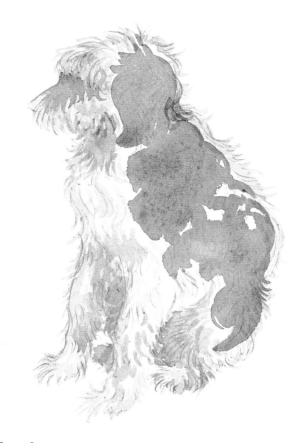

Stage 2

locks of white fur. So more masking fluid is added to protect this colour, and another medium-grey wash is then put on to the shadowed parts of the dog's face, head and body.

Stage 3

I make sure that the dog-shape is protected by masking fluid sufficiently far in from its edges to permit the background colour to be brushed on with considerable speed, and then prepare two mixtures of colour: one of manganese blue and a little Payne's grey, the other of Winsor violet, Payne's grey and a little ultramarine.

These are applied in bold free strokes, diagonally, in such a way as to let both colours be seen and to mix and, in places, to drag over the paper and let a little of it remain uncovered.

Stage 4 – the finished painting

It is essential that the work is allowed to dry thoroughly before the solidified masking fluid is rubbed off, otherwise it may damage the surface of the paper. When this was done, the dog was revealed, standing out cleanly against the background. A very dark bluish grey was used for some more shaggy locks on the grey parts of the body and ear, and the black end of the nose added.

This treatment has the quite pleasing effect of giving the picture the appearance of a print.

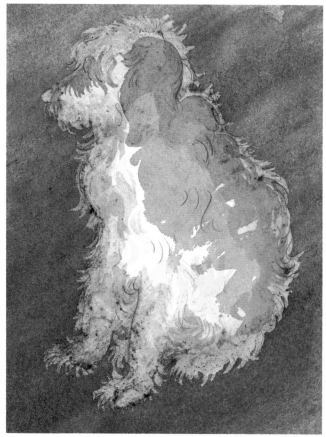

Stage 3

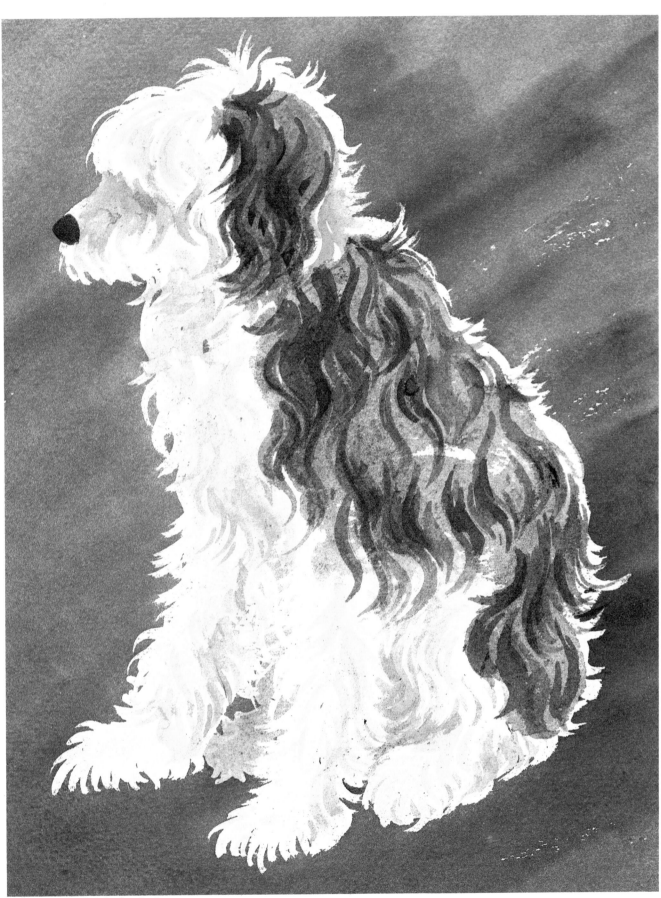

Stage 4 – the finished painting

Greyhounds

Greyhounds are another very ancient group, bred for coursing – running down hunted animals, however swift – and capable of considerable speeds. Our own racing greyhounds show clearly the shape of the dogs: salukis, Afghan hounds, borzois, Irish wolfhounds and Scottish deerhounds are very like them under their hair, and whippets and Italian greyhounds are smaller versions of the same animal.

They are well proportioned, graceful dogs, strong, and deep-chested – essential to accommodate large powerful lungs.

The member of the group illustrated below is a saluki, the Persian greyhound, said to be scarcely changed in 5000 years. This individual has a pale creamy colour, smooth and shiny, with long wavy hair on the ears and tail, and fringes on legs and feet. A smooth thin wash is used for the body, the form indicated with deeper tones; a thin black wash over the muzzle, and details of the face, eye and nose; then wavy brush marks for the long locks of hair on ears and tail.

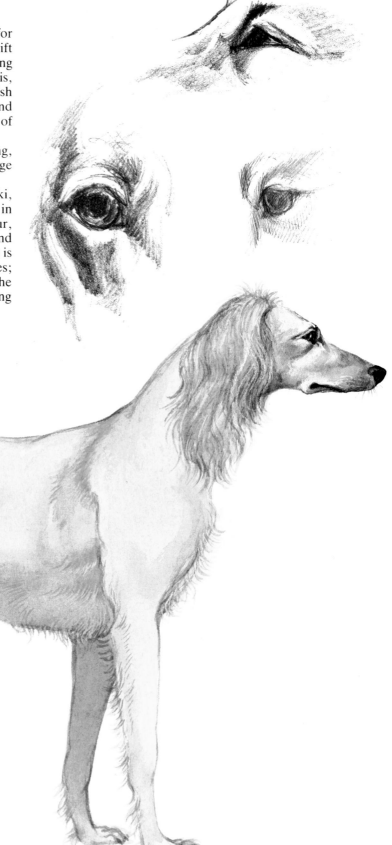

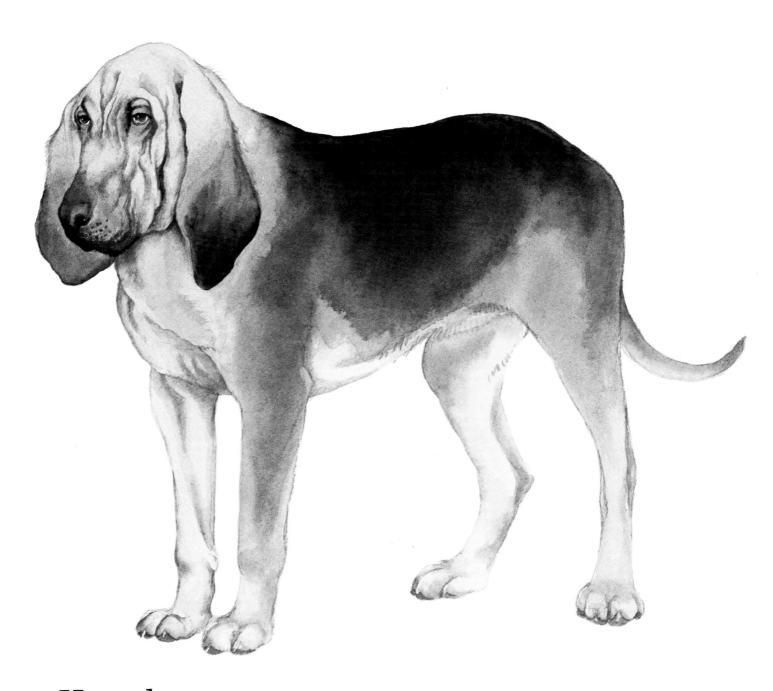

Hounds

One tends to count as one group a number of dogs called hounds of various kinds, which are used in packs to hunt their quarry by scent: bloodhounds, foxhounds, harriers, beagles, basset and other hounds, used for hunting foxes, hares, otters and anything else that will run far enough. Bloodhounds were originally used for hunting deer and were brought over to this country by William of Normandy. They are used for finding people now, of course, and have the ability to follow a scent as much as four days old. This kind of fact reveals how completely different from ours is a dog's sensitivity to smells.

The most complicated part of this drawing is the bloodhound's face with its swags and folds of skin.

Apart from this it is a matter of an all-over wash of light yellowish brown, with black washed over it after it is dry, and a stronger mixture of brown to define the modelling of legs, feet and body.

Golden retrievers

Original size: 358 × 530mm/14¼ × 21¼in.
Paper: Saunders 300gsm/140lb.

Here we have two large dogs to combine into an acceptable composition – they are Golden retrievers, half-brothers, though not particularly alike in face or colour. The best arrangement seemed to be one dog sitting upright and the other lying down, both looking in the same direction. This L-shaped composition filled out the space sufficiently without overwhelming it.

A feature of this breed is the long, glossy bright-coloured coat, very thick and red-gold in colour.

Many studies are made of the two dogs, in any attitude they happen to assume as I draw. This is necessary, since it is essential to become familiar with their appearance as individuals as well as examples of the breed. The result of this work is a number of pages of drawings of both details and complete figures, some in postures fairly close to what I require for the picture, some quite different. I have studies of paws, hair patterns, facial features and other details. From all this material I then work out the composition of my picture, drawing on all the information contained in the studies and on memory. I then refer again to the dogs to check the accuracy of my work, and to give authenticity to my portrait of the pair. It will be seen that the individual characters of both are clearly differentiated. The differences are not great, but careful study of the animals while one works on the finished drawing reveals the differences quite clearly. Washes of pale golden brown are put over the figures, varied with additions of more burnt sienna in places to give a range of colour and tone which will show the glossy texture; details of the fur are added before the washes are fully dry.

A rather yellowish green is used for the grass on which the dogs are lying, to keep the whole rather high

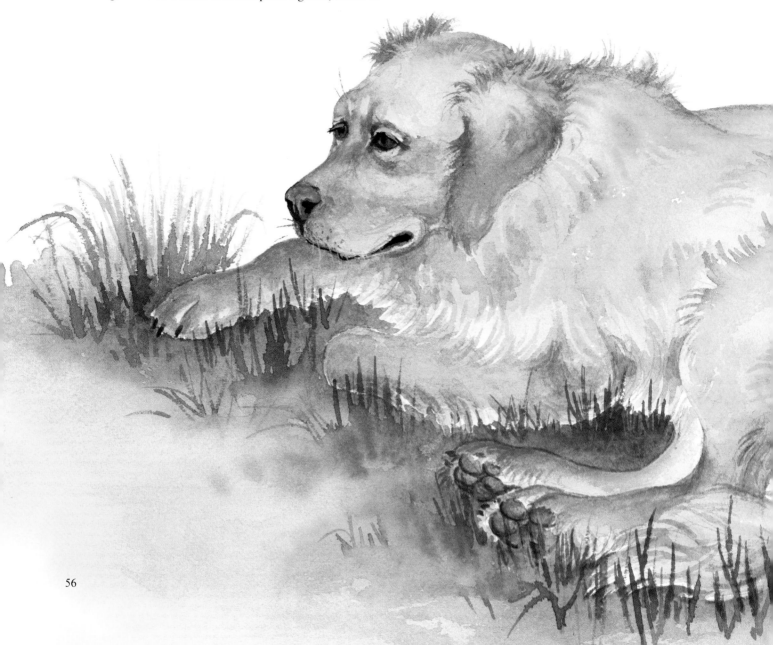

in tone; also it is in keeping with the yellow-brown of the dogs. The green is darkened with burnt sienna and black where it edges the dogs' bodies, partly to contrast, but also to give weight at the bottom of the picture.

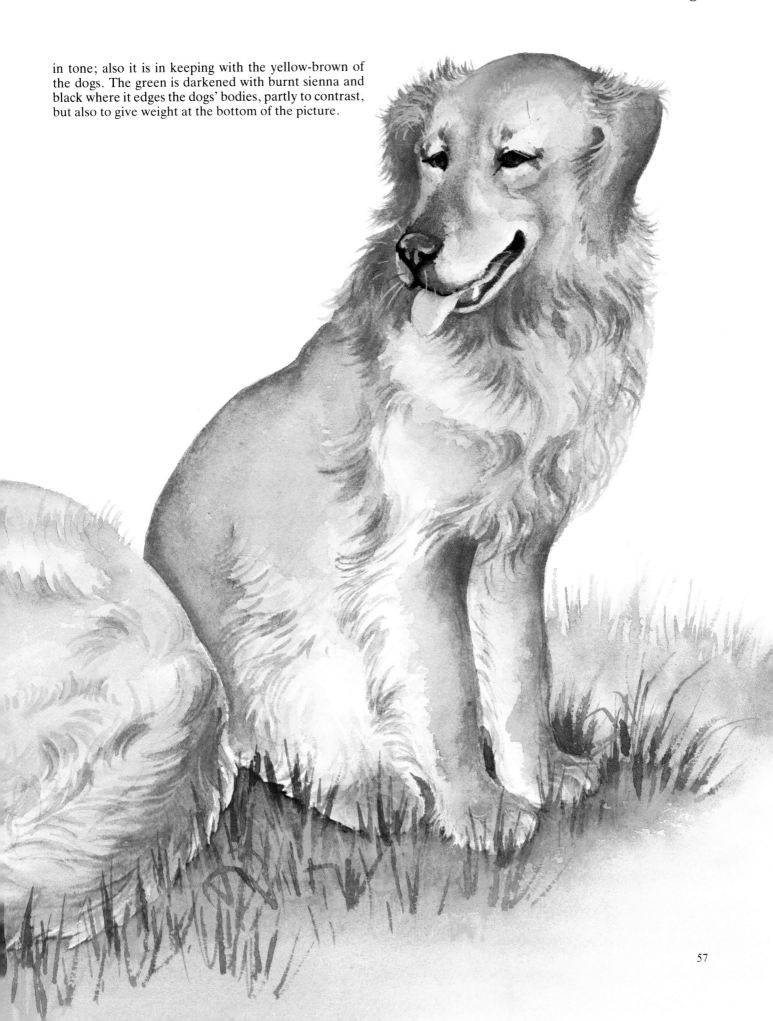

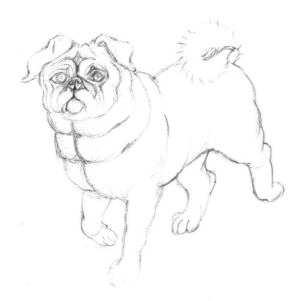

Stage 1

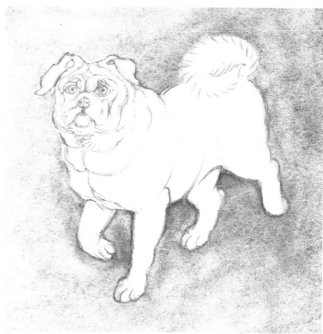

Stage 2

Pug: demonstration

Original size: 225mm sq./9in. sq.
Paper: Saunders 300gsm/140lb.

Stage 1

This painting has a simple wash background, as I do not want to distract attention from the complications of the folds of skin on the dog's head and shoulders. These must be carefully drawn before one starts to put on the colour.

Stage 2

The background is wetted with clean water, and the colour applied – a mixture of blues: manganese, cobalt and ultramarine – light around the head, darker where it adjoins the lighter-toned body.

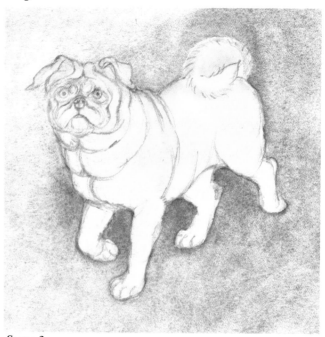

Stage 3

Stage 3

A very pale wash of yellow ochre is put over the whole dog; some stronger yellow ochre is added along its back and on its tail.

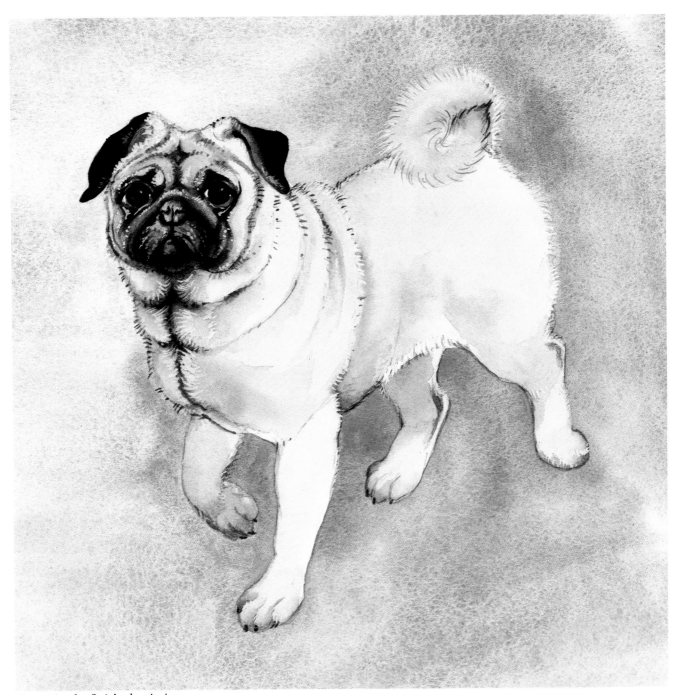

Stage 4 – the finished painting

Stage 4 – the finished painting

A thin wash of black over the yellow ochre gives some modelling to the body and legs, and the rolls of loose skin around the shoulders and neck. This is built up in stages to a full-strength black, to define the folds on the face and the black mask and ears, and the eyes, in which a little burnt sienna and black has been used for the irises.

Opaque white mixed with a little yellow ochre and black is used to define the fur on face, chest and abdomen. A light opaque grey then defines the details of nose and mouth, and the folds around the eyes. A touch of almost pure white outside the irises helps to enhance the characteristically worried expression.

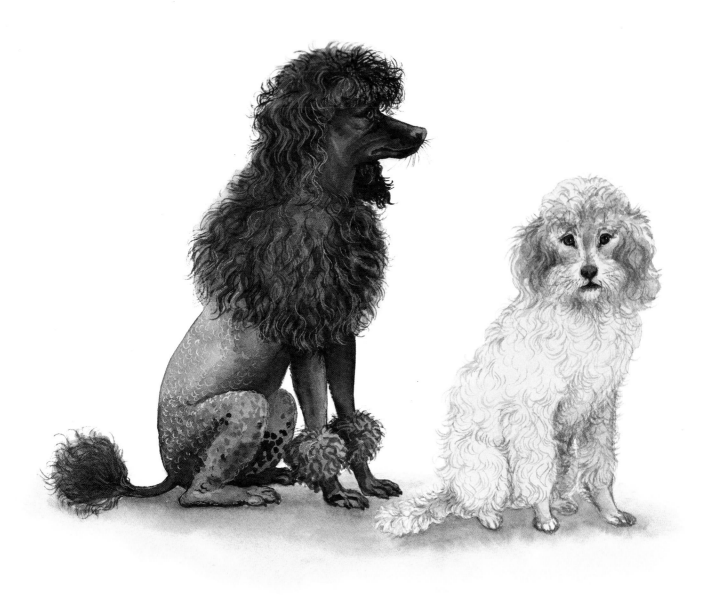

Domestic breeds

Complete classification of domestic dogs into groups is impossible; there are so many breeds whose ancestry is not known, and others whose forebears have come from more than one group, as in the case of the bull terrier, a mixture of bulldog and terrier (probably the old English white terrier). Often, when it is felt desirable to modify some feature in a breed, the change is brought about by introducing a strain of another breed which displays the desired characteristic. For example, the pointer was originally a rather slow, heavy dog; with the development of quick-firing guns it became desirable to have a swift-mover, so some fox-hound blood was bred into the breed.

Poodles are a breed which is not easy to classify with certainty. Originating in Germany, they were used for sheep herding and for retrieving waterfowl, and came to be used for this purpose over much of Europe, so

that their function was the same as a water spaniel's.

The practice of clipping poodles' coats into patterns originated as a means of reducing interference with their movements in water, and of keeping them warm when they emerged. Since those more practical times, man has given full scope to his taste for topiary, and devised many fanciful variations on the theme; two are shown in the picture, a standard and a miniature poodle; the larger, black one's waves and curls are put in over a soft wash of medium black, softened at the edges, with many fine brush strokes in black and then, using opaque white, in pale grey. The little dog has his curls in similar strokes, but all in a colour slightly deeper in tone than his ground colour. As always, with a long-haired dog, when I work on the preliminary drawing, I draw the inner dog first, and build out the thickness of the hair over this.

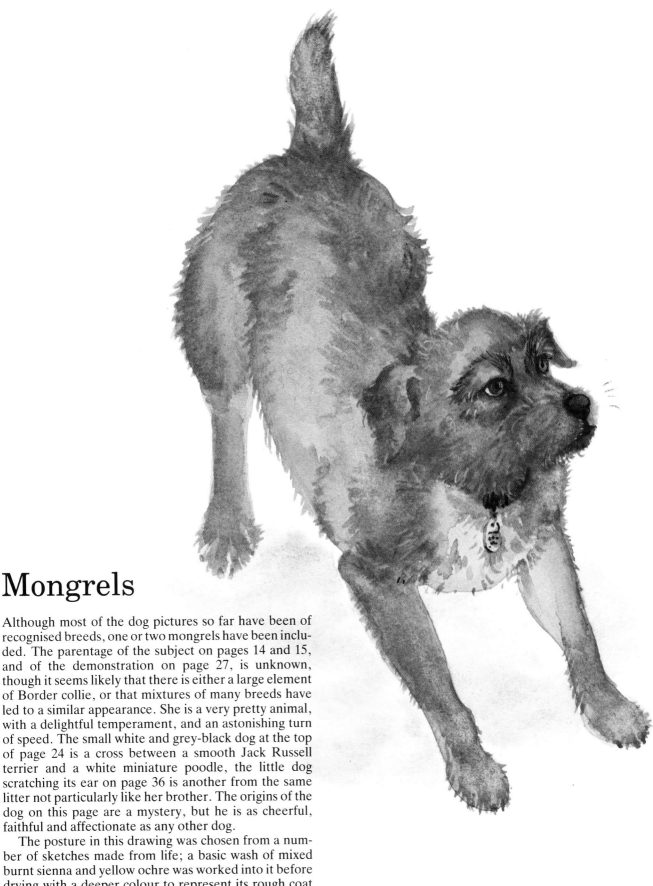

Mongrels

Although most of the dog pictures so far have been of recognised breeds, one or two mongrels have been included. The parentage of the subject on pages 14 and 15, and of the demonstration on page 27, is unknown, though it seems likely that there is either a large element of Border collie, or that mixtures of many breeds have led to a similar appearance. She is a very pretty animal, with a delightful temperament, and an astonishing turn of speed. The small white and grey-black dog at the top of page 24 is a cross between a smooth Jack Russell terrier and a white miniature poodle, the little dog scratching its ear on page 36 is another from the same litter not particularly like her brother. The origins of the dog on this page are a mystery, but he is as cheerful, faithful and affectionate as any other dog.

The posture in this drawing was chosen from a number of sketches made from life; a basic wash of mixed burnt sienna and yellow ochre was worked into it before drying with a deeper colour to represent its rough coat and structure on the head and legs. Once this was dry the nose, eyes, collar and address tag were added.

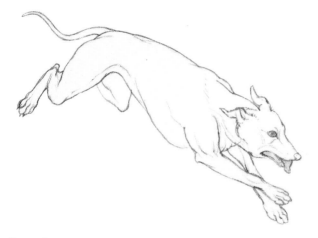

Stage 1

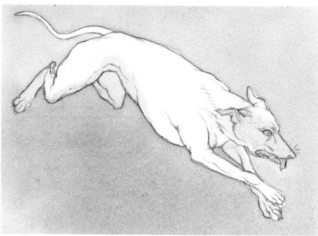

Stage 2

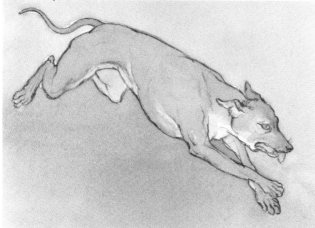

Stage 3

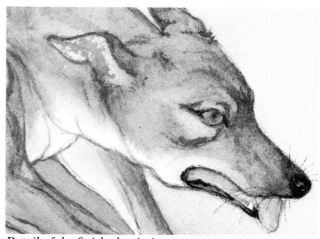

Detail of the finished painting

Running greyhound: demonstration

Original size: 160 × 225mm/6½ × 9in.
Paper: Mould-made Whatman 300gsm/140lb.

Stage 1

This is another subject where careful drawing must be the first consideration. A pencil outline has been used, and the background kept very simple.

Photographic reference has been used to ensure accuracy. The tongue is coloured with a thin wash of cadmium scarlet, and the eye with yellow ochre.

Stage 2

The background of pale yellow-green, mixed from pthalocyanine blue and cadmium lemon, is floated on to the previously wetted paper. Stronger green, with a little Payne's grey added, is put into the wet wash below the figure of the dog.

A very weak wash of yellow ochre, with a very little burnt sienna, is put over the face, the inside of the further legs, the belly, the front of the nearer thigh, and the dog's right hind foot.

Stage 3

At this stage the main colour of the dog's coat is added, using a stronger wash of yellow ochre, and blending this colour where it ends with the very pale parts already done, so that there are no hard edges between the dark and pale parts.

Detail

This detail of the greyhound painting shows how bones, tendons and even blood-vessels show through the thin, close coat of the animal, just as they do in a thoroughbred horse. This has been conveyed by the application of darker, more sharply-edged patches of tone than those used for the broader forms on which these details lie.

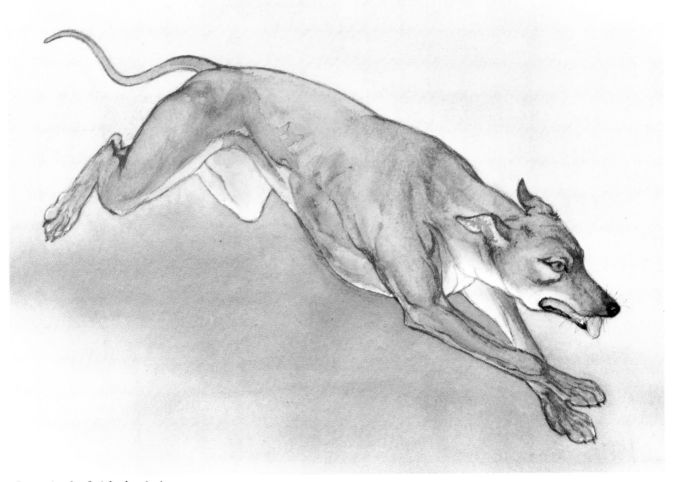

Stage 4 – the finished painting

Stage 4 – the finished painting

The final building up of deep tones is done at this stage with successive washes of almost pure burnt sienna, and of black on the muzzle, neck, chest, thigh and feet. The muscles and veins are defined, and yet stronger black used for pupil, mouth, nose, whiskers and claws. Details of ears, eyes and feet are strengthened, and the pencil line built up in places with a black wash line.

Painting animals in watercolour

In making studies, it is often necessary to concentrate on the overall posture and proportions of the animal, rather than on the detailed structure of noses, ears and eyes. Separate small drawings are then made to show the exact construction of these features, and it is interesting to compare the variations in the different breeds. The drawings below compare the degrees of development of the folded skin around the jaws of buhund (top), spaniel (right, middle) and mastiff (bottom right); the widely differing ears of the buhund and of the spaniel and bassethound (bottom, centre) with the greater length and weight of their upper part; and the varied looseness of the folded skin around the eyes of the bassethound, St. Bernard and bloodhound (all bottom, left).

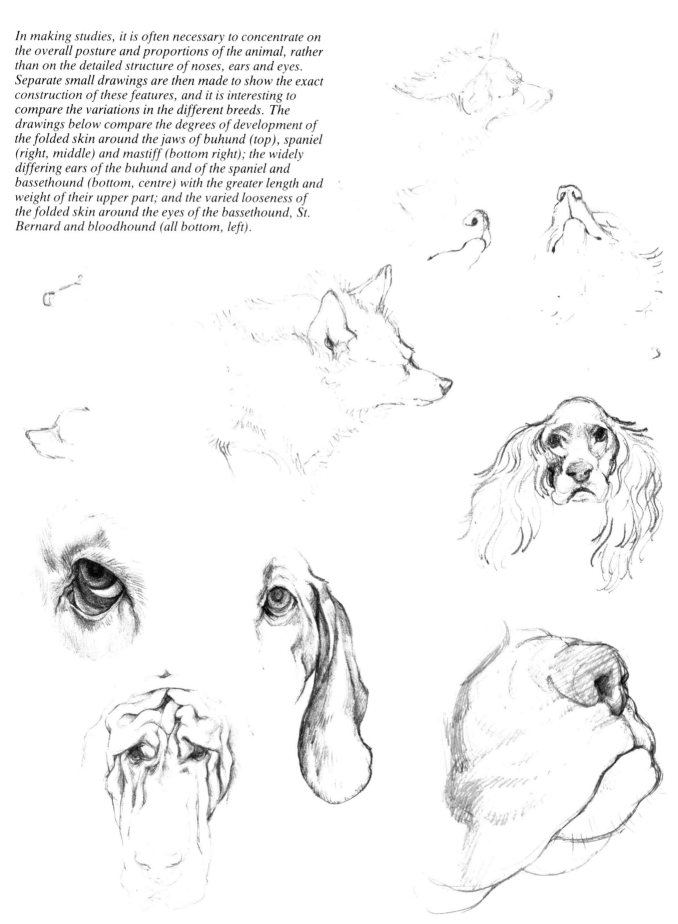

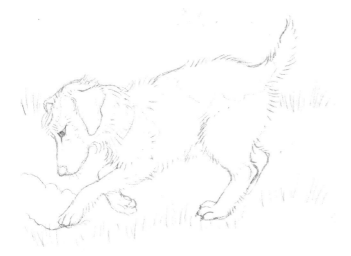

Stage 1

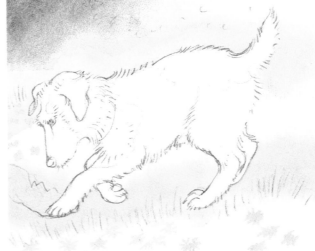

Stage 2

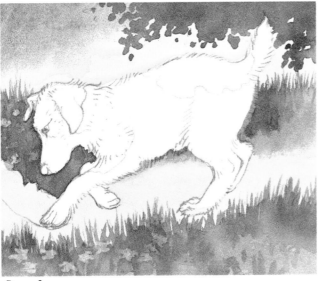

Stage 3

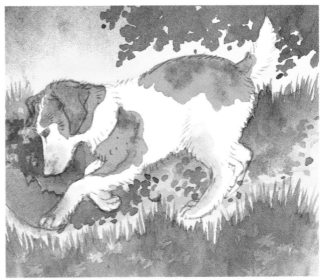

Stage 4

Dog, digging: demonstration

Original size: 180 × 220mm/7 × 8⅝in.
Paper: Saunders 180gsm/90lb.

This picture again uses masking solution but to a lesser extent than in the Old English sheepdog painting.

The way in which I use it is a little different; it again defines the edges of the animal, so that a wash can be put freely over the background, leaving a clean edge, and leaving the brown and white dog to stand out against the green and sandy-coloured setting, yet defining the character of the subject's coat. The short, rough coat seems best conveyed by the use of fine brush marks, in brown and grey on pale yellow-brown and white patches of hair, and also, by using opaque white, with a counter-change of tone, pale yellowish and white brush strokes on these dark and middle-toned areas.

Stage 1

The dog (that most dedicated digger, a Jack Russell terrier) is drawn carefully, and the features of the background only lightly indicated. With all these pictures, the animals have been very carefully drawn beforehand, often more than once, and the final result carefully traced so that the drawing can be reproduced without harming the delicate surface of the paper.

I then apply the masking fluid all round the edges of the animal, with indications of hairs where these interrupt the outline, as on the head, neck, tail and elbow.

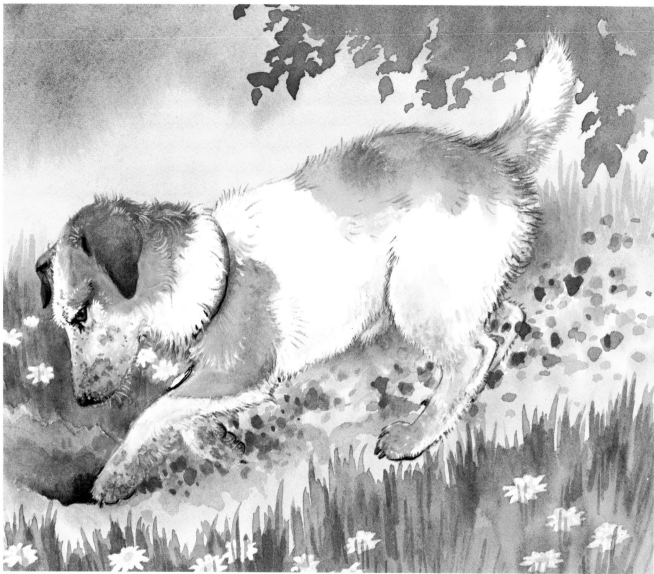

Stage 5 – the finished painting

Stage 2

The daisies in the grass are then stopped out, and all this work with masking fluid is then allowed to dry thoroughly before I embark on the painting of the background. The far background is painted into wet paper – a pale lemon wash with a hint of phthalocyanine blue, above it a dull green obtained by adding Payne's grey. While this dries, space can be left for the patch of grass behind the dog, and a ground of yellow ochre with burnt umber washed across at the level of the dog's feet.

Stage 3 and 4

A deeper yellow-green (cadmium lemon, phthalocyanine blue, and burnt sienna) is blobbed on for the overhanging foliage in the top right-hand corner, and, slightly watered down, used also for the two grassy areas – the detail of the grass is added with a darker mixture, and little variations of colour are made with touches of yellow and extra blue in the mixture.

When the background is absolutely dry, the masking fluid is removed from the edges of the dog's shape. A yellow ochre/burnt sienna wash, stronger than the brown-yellow ground, is put on to the dog's patches, inside the hole, and around his feet for the lumps of soil.

Stage 5 – the finished painting

The black and grey detail of eye, nose, ears and paws, and quite a lot of elaborate work on the outline of the animal, defining the growth of hair and the smoother forms of the legs, are now added. Some paler grey is used to indicate shapes on the head, body and leg, and at this stage I add the brush marks defining the hair.

The masking fluid is now removed from the background, leaving the daisies sharply defined in the grass. Yellow centres are added, and a few blades of grass allowed to grow up in front of some of them.

CATS

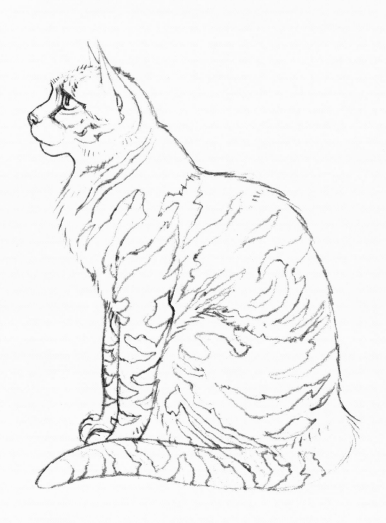

Cats

Cats are perhaps the best subject for an aspiring animal painter to start on. Even if you do not have one of your own, other people's cats seem to spend many hours contemplating the world from garden walls, doorsteps and pavements. Often they are friendly and approachable enough to permit stroking and head rubbing, which will help you to increase your knowledge of their structure.

If you have a cat of your own, it probably spends plenty of time sleeping, and this will present you with an ideal subject on which to practise.

Whereas dogs vary enormously in size and shape, cats are very much alike in these respects – there is variation, but within much narrower limits than with dogs. There is considerable variety of colour and pattern, however, some of which is shown on these two pages and the previous one. The plain colours include black, white, brown, beige and blue-grey. The patterns include: blotched, striped and spotted tabbies; every possible variation of random patches of black and white; pale with dark face, tail and legs; patches of tabby on white, and variations of colour of the tabby pattern, from grey and brown through a large range of orange, red, yellow and apricot. More complicated still is the tortoiseshell, the pattern of which is an arrangement of random patches of white, black, and red tabby, which can be either the blotched or the striped tabby pattern. These may be mixed in any proportion, and can be very muddled and hard to sort out, but it is not safe to make up a tortoiseshell pattern unless you thoroughly understand the underlying principle.

The illustrations show a black and white cat, with a fairly common arrangement of the two colours, a ginger (red tabby), a blue (this one is a Blue Persian, but the colour occurs in short-haired cats as well), a white, and a tortoiseshell. There are of course many others; one can only pick out a few examples to illustrate some of the colour varieties.

The differences in conformation among domestic cats are dealt with later in this chapter, but it may be interest-

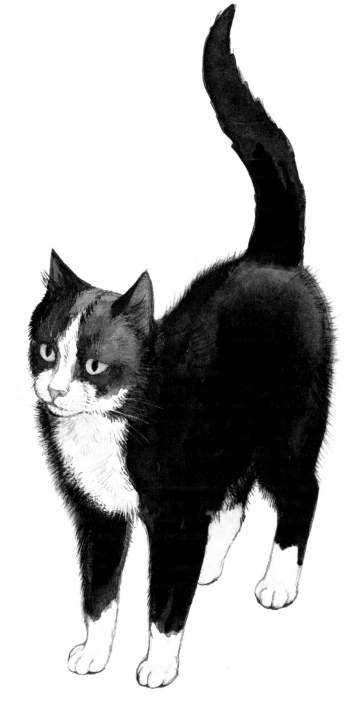

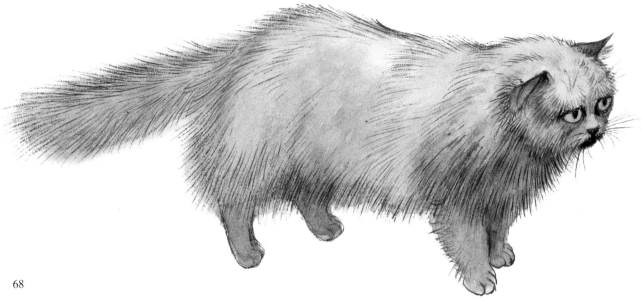

ing to consider how consistent is the conformation of all the wild cats. Apart from extreme differences in size, with tigers at one end of the scale and the little black-footed cat at the other (slightly smaller than the average domestic cat), the shape of the whole family of Felidae is extremely consistent; some have shorter legs than others, or wider heads, or shorter faces, but the differences are less than in many other families. Lions and tigers look very different, partly because of the difference in colour and pattern, and particularly because of the presences of the mane and tail tuft in lions, but under their skins the two are indistinguishable, though I believe that the largest tigers (the Siberian ones) can reach a size greater than lions. This may be because the biggest tigers are those found furthest north, while the lion's range is greatly restricted, particularly in its northern parts, so perhaps all the really large lions have become extinct; tigers in the extreme south of their range are considerably smaller than their northern relations.

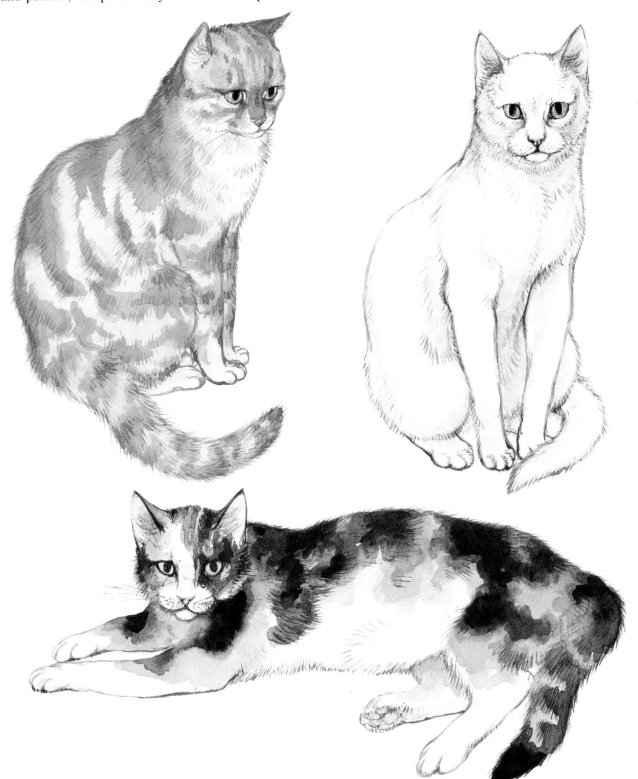

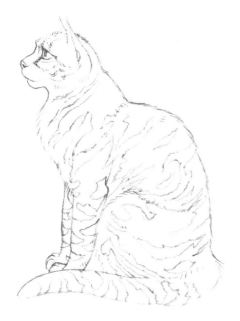

Stage 1

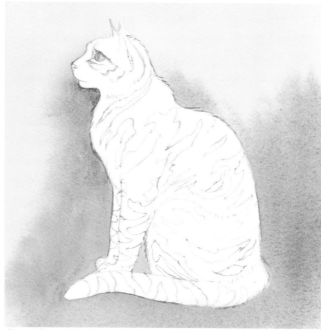

Stage 2

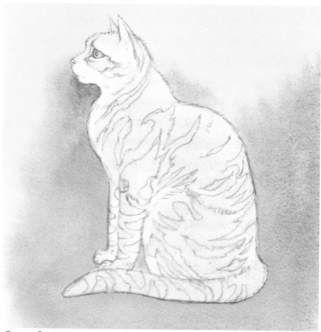

Stage 3

Tabby cat: demonstration

Original size: 225mm sq./9in. sq.
Paper: Saunders Not 300gsm/140lb.

The cat chosen for this demonstration, a striped silver tabby, is strikingly marked, so I have decided to present a straightforward side view, and provide a contrast in colour by means of a simple wash background.

Stage 1

The drawing is quite a complicated one in that the pattern of the cat's coat is the main feature of the composition and must be drawn accurately. As these patterns obey certain rules, although showing variations, it is desirable for the markings to be clearly indicated at this stage in order to be finished correctly later.

Stage 2

The background is wetted thoroughly with clean water, nearly up to the edges of the cat, but not quite reaching them. This is in order to prevent the water, and, later, the background colour spreading over the edges. When the wash of yellow (cadmium light) is put on to the wet background, again not right up to the edge of it (so that there is no risk of a dry edge where you do not want it), it is finished with a finer brush and the colour taken carefully up to the outline of the animal. While the yellow background is still damp, a mixture of cadmium red light

and burnt sienna is dropped into it where the orange is required. The yellow of the eye, and the pink nose and ears can also be put in at this stage.

Stage 3

When all the work done so far is absolutely dry, a very pale grey wash is applied over the figure of the cat, and this in turn is allowed to dry thoroughly.

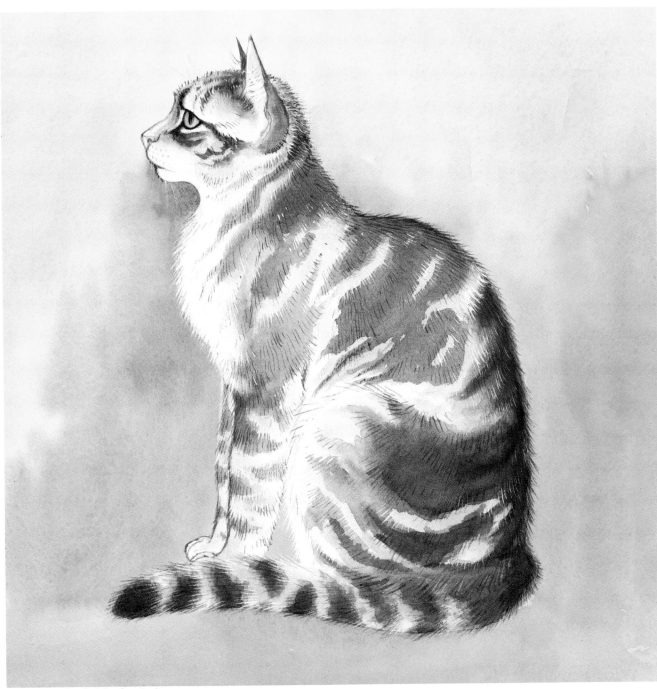

Stage 4 – the finished painting

Stage 4 – the finished painting

The markings of the cat's coat are now added, with a strong lamp black wash; this should be made simpler by all the work and care spent on the drawing. The edges of the markings should be softened where pale fur merges into black. The picture is finished with such details as the fur, the pupil of the eye, and whiskers.

Cat conformation

Although the differences in build between one type of cat and another are not very great, there are nevertheless three distinct types into which cat-breeders divide them:

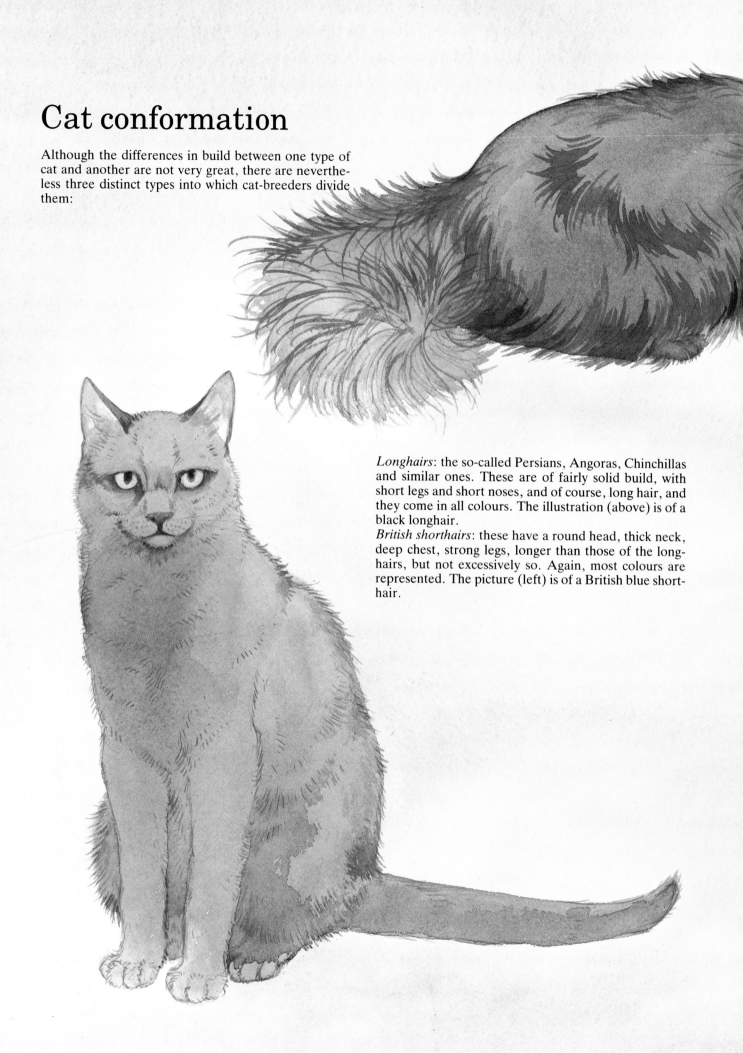

Longhairs: the so-called Persians, Angoras, Chinchillas and similar ones. These are of fairly solid build, with short legs and short noses, and of course, long hair, and they come in all colours. The illustration (above) is of a black longhair.

British shorthairs: these have a round head, thick neck, deep chest, strong legs, longer than those of the longhairs, but not excessively so. Again, most colours are represented. The picture (left) is of a British blue shorthair.

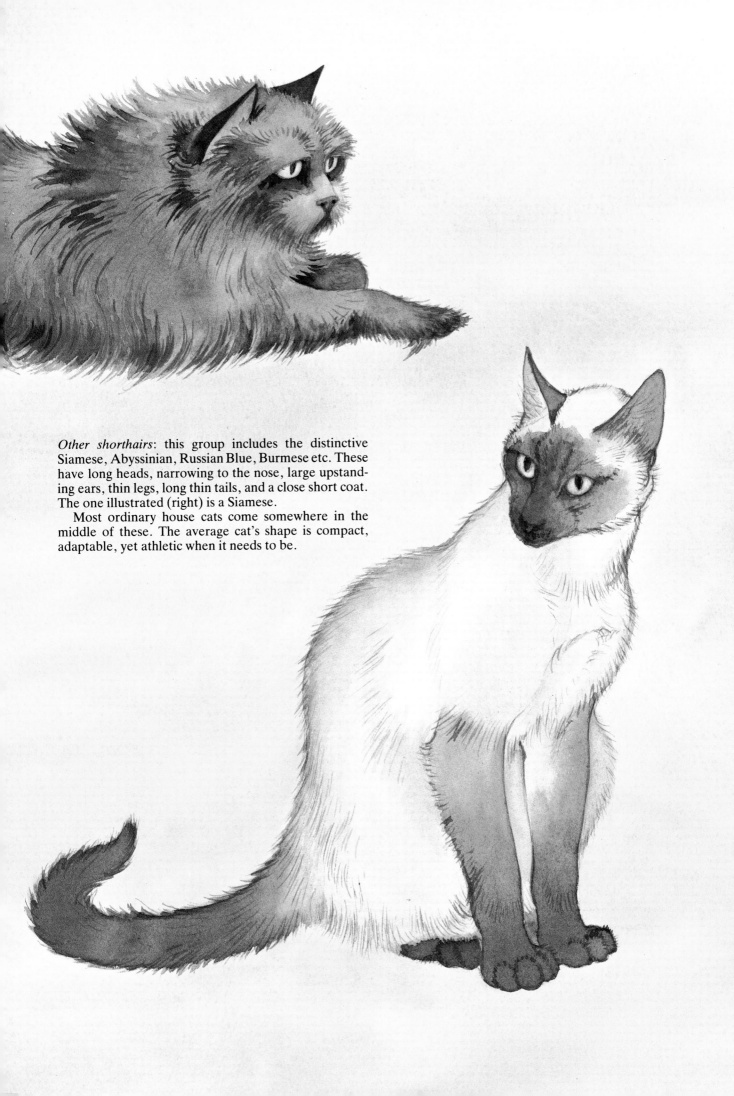

Other shorthairs: this group includes the distinctive Siamese, Abyssinian, Russian Blue, Burmese etc. These have long heads, narrowing to the nose, large upstanding ears, thin legs, long thin tails, and a close short coat. The one illustrated (right) is a Siamese.

Most ordinary house cats come somewhere in the middle of these. The average cat's shape is compact, adaptable, yet athletic when it needs to be.

Tabby patterns

There are two distinct kinds of tabby pattern, striped and blotched. They are quite different from each other, and never appear both on the same coat. The striped tabby pattern – which may vary in the length of the stripes, so that some cats have stripes broken up into short pieces that could be described as spots rather than stripes – is very close to the patterns of some of the wild cats. I once had a cat which was almost identical in markings to the African Fettered Cat or Caffre Cat, Felis Lybica, which will interbreed with domestic cats. These markings have considerable beauty, and provide wonderful camouflage. My striped tabby, sitting under shrubs on a sunny day, was practically invisible from four feet away.

The blotched tabby pattern (opposite) has no counterpart in the wild, and is presumably a mutation of the striped tabby pattern. It is now the more common type of tabby, in Britain at any rate. It is a difficult pattern to draw as, although it seems to be random, it is virtually impossible to make up convincingly. It is always worth taking the trouble to draw it carefully from an actual cat.

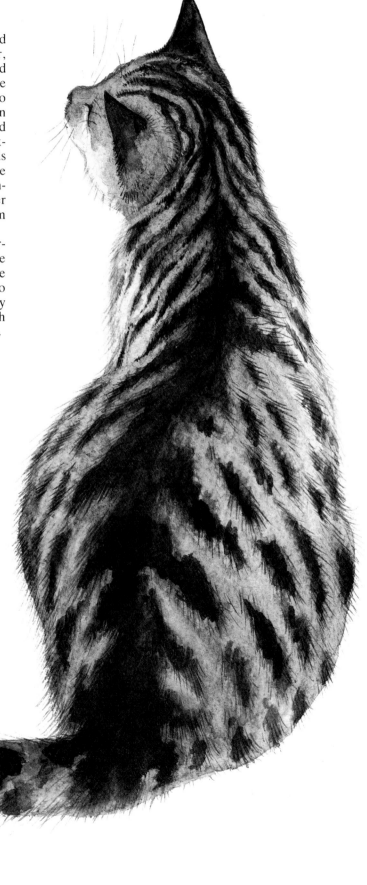

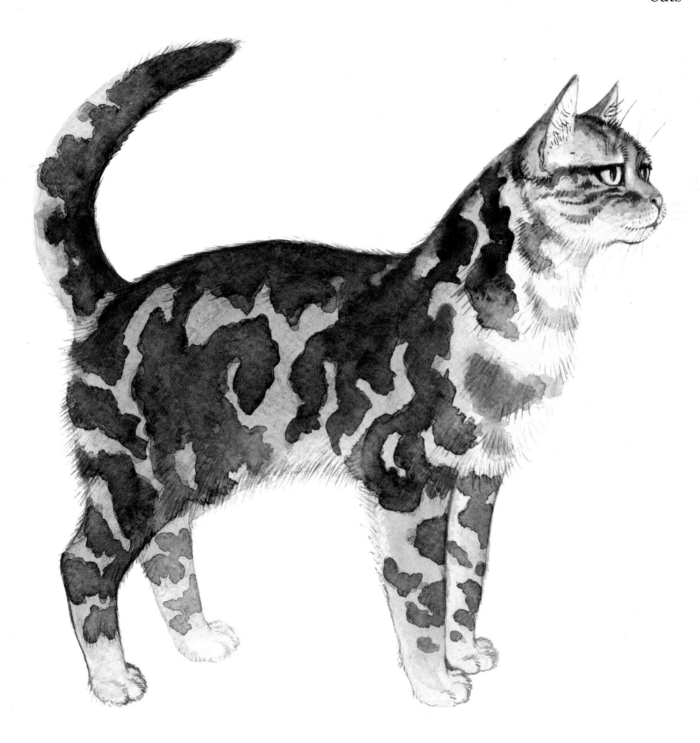

Siamese cat: demonstration

Original size: 290 × 222mm/11½ × 8¾in.
Paper: Mould-made Whatman 410gsm/200lb.

Stage 1 (page 76)
The cat is drawn in the allotted space, and needs fairly careful placing, since the figure spans almost the whole depth of the picture and comes very close to its edges.

Stage 2 (page 76)
The whole background is wetted with clean water, and blue washes, pale above (a weak mixture of manganese blue and cobalt blue) and dark below (a mixture of phthalocyanine, ultramarine and a little black), where it will counter-change with the pale body of the animal. These blues have been mixed to tone with the brilliant blue of the cat's eyes. These are filled in with a strong bright mixture of cobalt and manganese blues; when this is almost dry, a drop of clean water is dripped into the middle, and mopped out with a squeezed-out brush – this gives depth and transparency to the eyes.

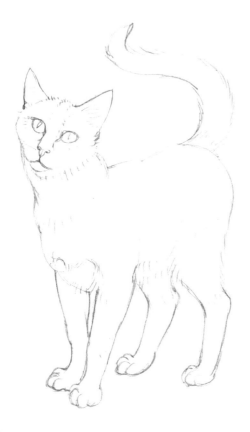

Stage 1

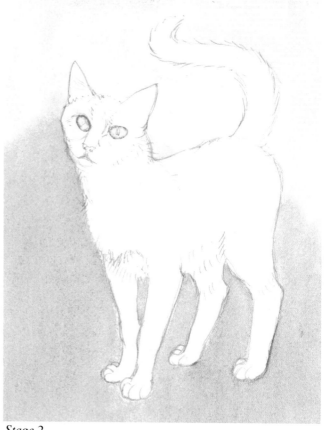

Stage 2

Stage 3

A pale wash (a very little yellow ochre and phthalo-cyanine blue, and a little black) is put over the whole cat. A wash of black with a little yellow ochre is put over the legs, tail, ears and face, washed out to merge into the light parts. A stronger yellow ochre and black wash than the pale ground colour is used to strengthen the fur colour on chest, throat and legs.

Stage 4 – the finished painting (page 77)

A fine brush and near-black is used to define the eyes, mouth, nose and ears, and for the vertical pupils.

Opaque white is mixed with a very small amount of yellow ochre and black, and used extensively to brush in fine hairs on the head and body, ears and whiskers, and in a darker mixture on the legs and to draw the toes.

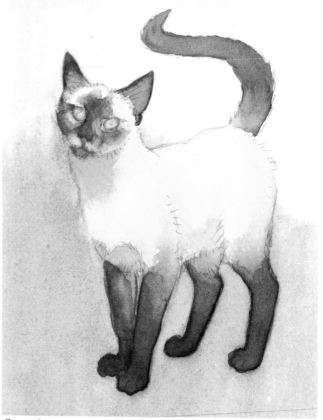

Stage 3

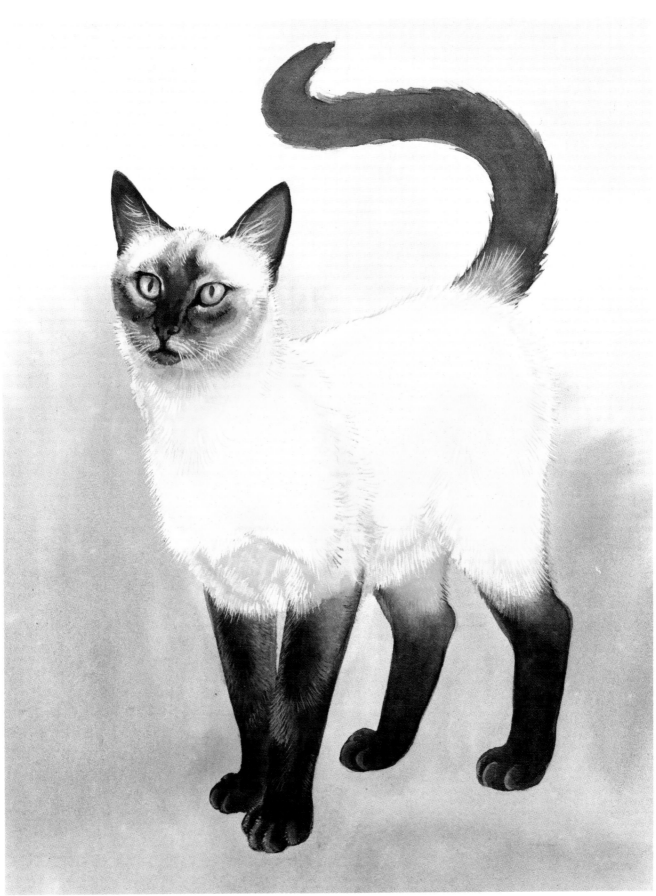

Stage 4 – the finished painting

Kittens

New kittens show considerable differences in proportion from adult cats. If attention is not paid to these differences, and their exact nature, it is difficult to draw kittens convincingly. It is difficult anyway, since they move so quickly and so suddenly.

I have made some drawings of kittens' heads and of complete kittens, which may shed some light on their characteristics and the way they develop from new-born infant to adolescent. It is surprising what a difference paying attention to these details makes – for example, having whiskers of the right length immediately establishes that you are drawing a kitten of a particular age.

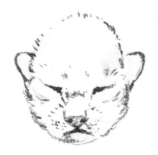

The new-born kitten, of course, has its eyes shut, and they stay shut until about ten days after birth. Usually they begin to open at the inner corner, and have a rather oriental look until they have unstuck completely. They are, like a human baby's eyes, a smokey blue, and change colour gradually to yellow, green, amber or clear blue. When the kitten is first born, its ears are very tiny, and far down at the sides of its head, the flap of the ear not being present. As the kitten grows, so do its ears, which appear to move up its head, although this apparent movement is really more a matter of the different size of the upper part of the ear in proportion to the lower part.

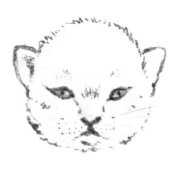

The whiskers are short and very fine at birth, of course, and they grow and coarsen as the fur grows; this also is sparse in a new kitten, which appears quite bald on its underside, muzzle and feet, though in fact the tiny soft hairs are present and quickly grow to an attractive coat of fluff. By the time a kitten is starting to leave the nursery for brief periods of play, the fur on the tail has grown sufficiently to give it the shape of a young fir tree – wide at the root and pointed at the tip.

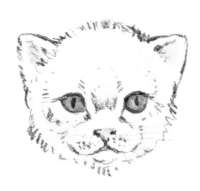

The nose and muzzle of a very new kitten appear proportionately large, which is not unreasonable considering the importance of the mouth and its use. There are no teeth, of course. As the face develops and the fur and ears grow, the characteristic chocolate-box prettiness of large bright forward-looking eyes, large ears, and small, delicately-formed, nose and mouth appears.

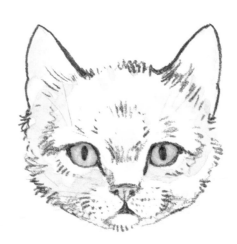

The body of the kitten shows similar changes; the new-born kittens have rather frog-like little legs, too weak to lift their bodies off the ground – they appear almost to be swimming as they move, and they spend a certain amount of time lying on their backs waving their legs slowly and helplessly until they manage to get the right way up. They grow quickly however, and within a few days of opening their eyes they are staggering, with legs spread wide and stomachs just off the floor, around their nest and, before long, finding their way to that part of the house where the food is kept. They very quickly begin to vary their diet from one of only their mother's milk. I once had a kitten which at five weeks or so would climb to the highest vantage point it could reach and scream for hand-outs of cheddar cheese.

Often the kittens are extremely active and adventurous before their mother is ready to let them go; and she will spend hours following her errant brood and carrying them one by one back to the nursery, each time she sets out for another kitten being overtaken by the one she has just deposited, on its way back to join its brothers and sisters. By this stage the kittens have changed completely from their infant state; they have become longer in the leg and their feet seem disproportionately big, and are extremely lively and active. By six months or so they will have reached adult size, though not yet as solid in the body or as serious in temperament as they will be in maturity.

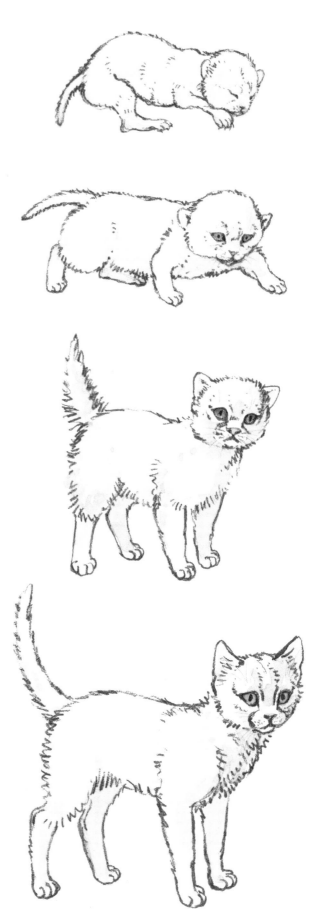

Capturing kittens at play

It is a pity to draw kittens only when they are asleep, or suckling, but as they move so quickly when they are playing they are a very difficult subject to catch. All the rules about drawing moving animals apply, but the postures assumed by kittens at play can be very surprising, and change rapidly. In addition more than one animal needs to be drawn, as they are most often playing in a group, jumping on each other and rolling over together. This makes it an advantage to use a piece of conté crayon or a wash brush – or a medium that produces a fuller mark than an ordinary pencil or drawing pen, so that one may depict the whole body and head instead of one edge of it. Such drawings can be used in conjunction with the more detailed measured drawings one can do from the sleeping animal and reference can also be made to photographs; these are particularly useful for checking proportions of one part of the animal compared to others. Such considerations are important for, if a mistake is made, the effect of the age of the kitten can be missed. If the head is too small, for example, it will look too old.

Most drawings you do of kittens at play will probably be unfinished, but they will be lively in a way that more carefully worked-out drawings rarely achieve; they are done in response to your direct and immediate reaction to what you see, and can form the basis of more considered work later on. It is not easy to do, but if you draw such subjects whenever the opportunity occurs, it will become progressively simpler.

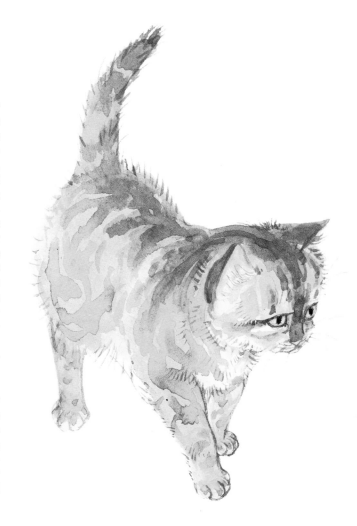

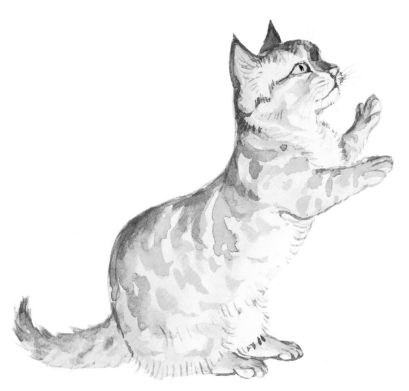

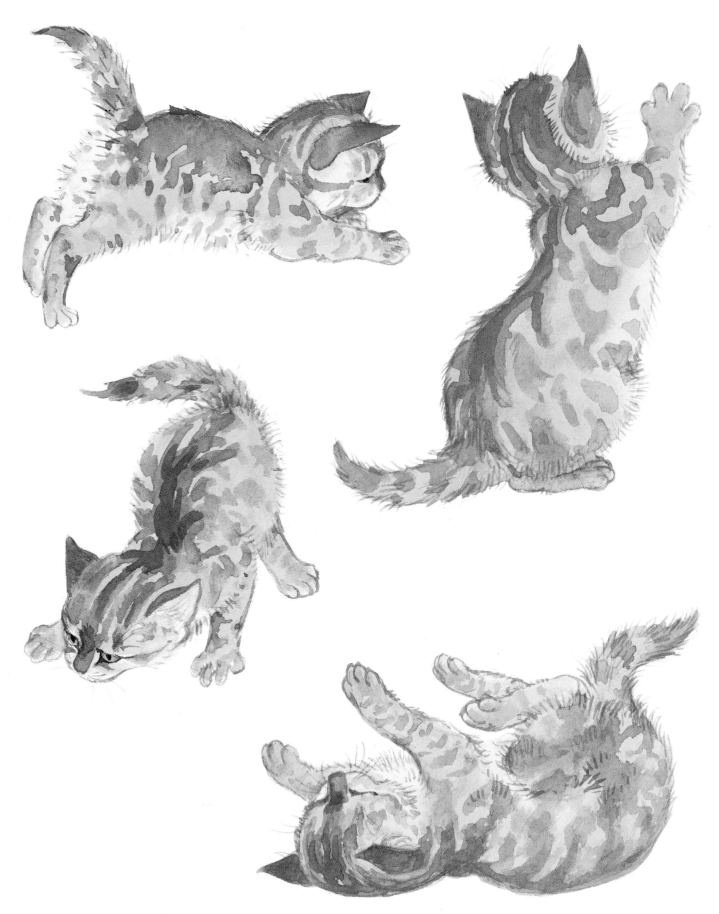

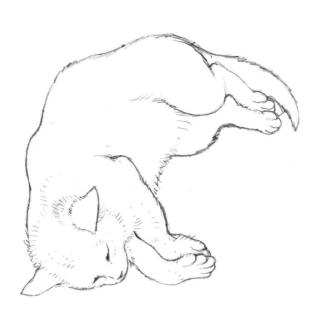

Stage 1

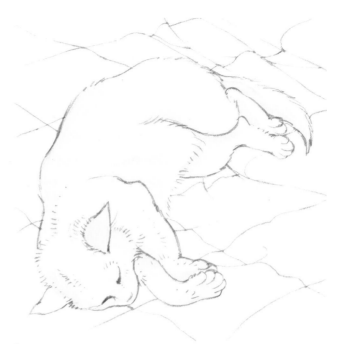

Stage 2

White cat on a colourful background: demonstration

Original size: 225mm sq./9in. sq.
Paper: Saunders Not 300gsm/140lb.

The purpose of this picture is to demonstrate how an interesting and colourful picture can be made by (after the drawing stage) concentrating one's efforts almost entirely on the background. It does not mean that time and attention is not spent on the drawing. On the contrary, the edges are so important in such a composition that, if anything, they need extra care.

Stage 1
Quite a long time was spent on this part of the picture; it is important that the perspective of the patchwork squares should be correct.

Stage 2
The cat is more or less completed at this stage, apart from the individual hairs which go over its outline. A pale pink is put on the nose and the edges of the ears, and a very pale yellow-grey used to indicate the modelling of head, paws and tail. The same, but a little darker, for defining details.

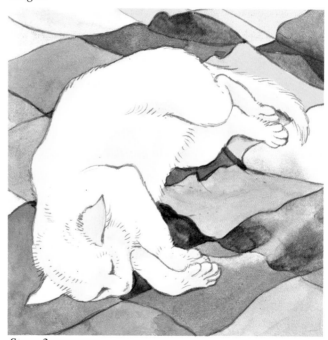

Stage 3

Stage 3
This stage, the most striking part of the picture, is simple to describe, but lengthy in execution. Each square in turn is washed with colour, and by means of blotting up colour or flooding in stronger pigment where required, the folds and rumples of the cloth are depicted. All the squares are green, blue, or purple, but great care has to be taken to maintain variety in these colours, so that the background is clearly a piece of genuine patchwork, not a mechanically repeated pattern.

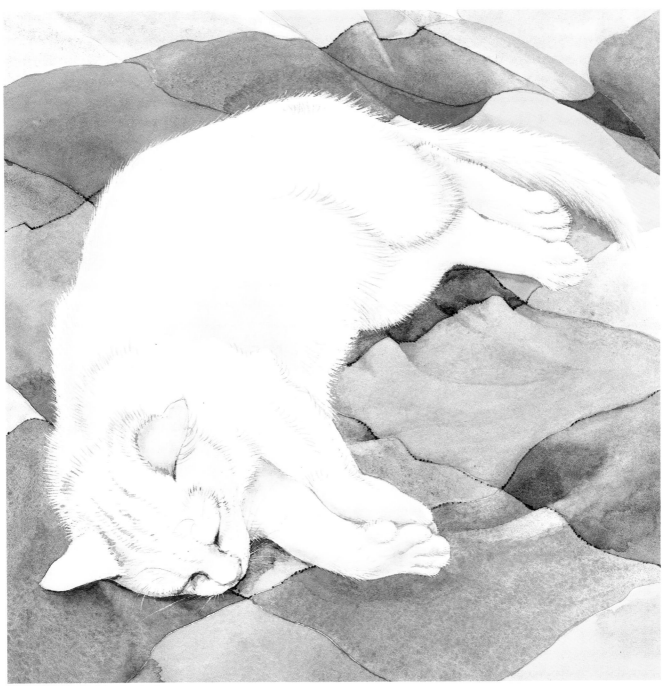

Stage 4 – the finished painting

Stage 4 – the finished painting

Small details complete the picture: hairs on the cat's edges (opaque white, and size 0 sable brush), whiskers, and tiny stitches on the seams of the patchwork.

    This theme lends itself to many interesting variations. I have given it the same kind of treatment in pastel, where the subject was a black animal and the picture done on black paper, and defined with a brightly-coloured background. A patterned rug, or richly-coloured embroidery could be substituted for the patchwork.

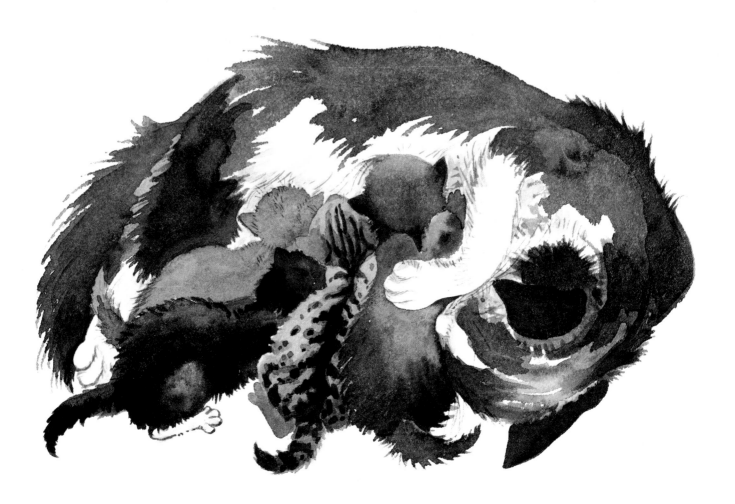

Cat with kittens

Original size: 170 × 230mm/6¾ × 9¼in.
Paper: Mould-made Saunders 180gsm/90lb.

A cat with a litter of small kittens makes an appealing picture. The subject has the advantage of being reasonably static, yet the small movements of the kittens' paws massaging the mother as they suckle prevent it from being too immobile. It can present a little difficulty in the drawing, as the kittens lie on top of or burrow underneath each other, and sometimes look like a mass of fur with a number of assorted, disconnected legs. However, careful observation and intelligent analysis of what you see is the important factor in drawing. Understanding is all; the marks you put down on paper will follow with comparative ease.

OTHER DOMESTIC ANIMALS AND BIRDS

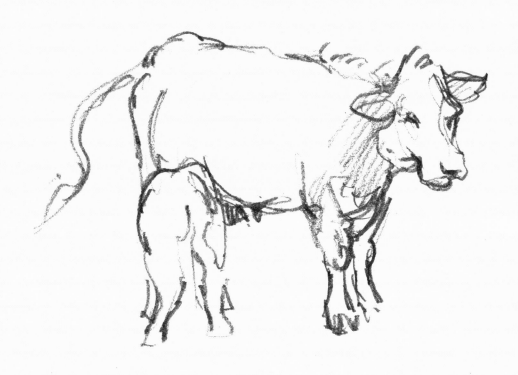

Other domestic animals and birds

Apart from dogs and cats, the animals which live in our homes include different creatures of many sorts such as guinea pigs, hamsters, mice, gerbils, and rabbits; canaries, budgerigars, parrots, and mynah birds; fish, tortoises, and stick insects.

There are many species of small mouse-like animals, and many of them look alike; obviously there are differences, but these are often minor, and are discovered in the course of the close examination which is so essential a part of any drawing, although the speed and suddenness of their movements can make such study difficult. The structure of their minute feet, the placing and direction of their often surprisingly long whiskers, the rich texture of their thick and colourful fur, and the size and shape of ears all need to be examined thoroughly – getting these things right is what will make your picture of an animal an unmistakable portrayal of an individual of a particular species.

These small creatures can be very timid and nervous; and they should only be handled if they are accustomed to it. When drawing these, or in fact any animals, be particularly careful about the eyes; so often what is

otherwise quite a reasonable drawing is spoiled because the eyes have been made too big, giving an unpleasant appearance of artificiality and 'cuteness'.

The mouse below right has settled into an almost spherical shape. This particular mouse is of course a common wild one, while the ones usually kept in the house are colour varieties of the house mouse. Hamsters, below, have become very popular in a few years. The gerbils opposite are a more recent enthusiasm, though the guinea pig, below, is a domestic pet of long standing.

Compare the handling of the paint in the guinea-pig and hamster pictures, where two completely contrasting kinds of fur are shown; the brush-strokes show the long wavy hair of the guinea-pig, while the areas of wash, darkening at the edges of the forms, but with little intervening delineation of texture depict the quite different, almost velvety character of the hamster's fur.

The method used for all of these studies is similar; careful drawing at first, a wash of the ground colour of the subject, built up with successive washes of colour to show graduations of colour and some modelling of the form, and an indication of hair patterns, and detailed features, added in completion. The treatment of these subjects is rather more free than many of the paintings earlier in the book.

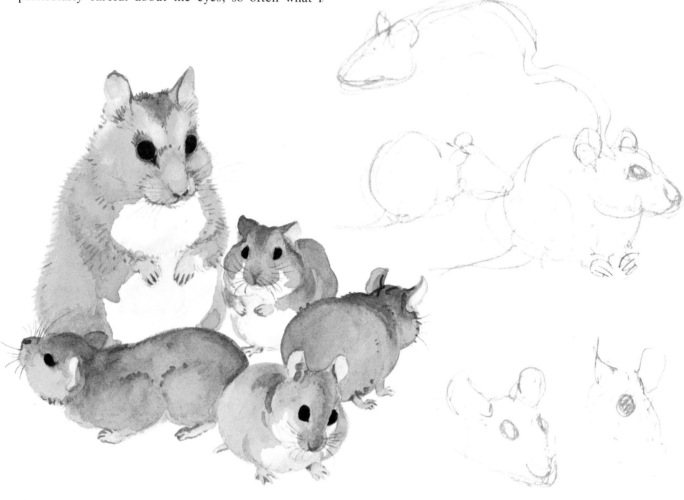

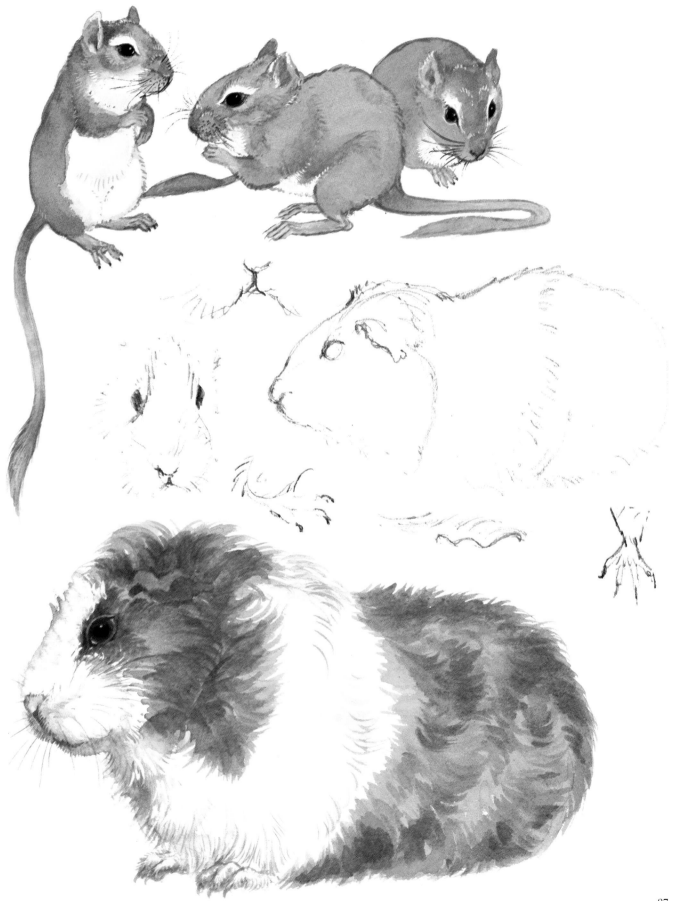

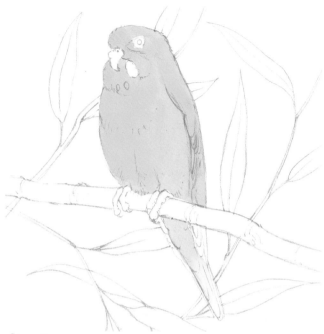

Stage 1

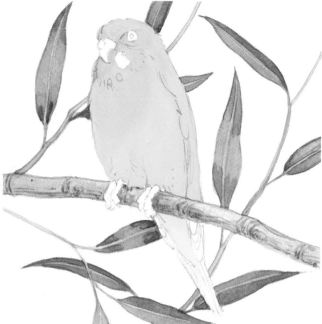

Stage 2

Budgerigar: demonstration

Original size: 225mm sq./9in. sq.
Paper: Mould-made Saunders 300gsm/140lb.

This is another painting with a complicated composition which has to be carefully worked out. The bird perches before a kind of all-over pattern of gum leaves and a lattice of stems.

Stage 1

The drawing is carefully transferred to the paper, and a strong wash of yellow (cadmium lemon warmed up with a little cadmium yellow) put on the whole bird except for the eye, beak, blue patch and feet, and the tip of the tail.

Stage 2

The branch, twigs and leaves are painted in pale washes: weak burnt sienna with a little yellow for the twigs; a greyish blue-green of yellow, Payne's grey and a touch of phthalocyanine blue for the leaves; a slightly brownish grey for the branch.

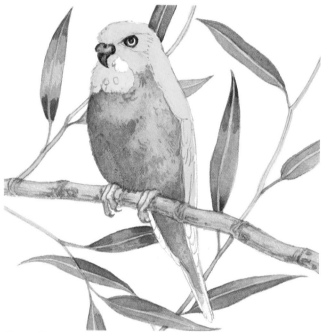

Stage 3

Stage 3

A thin wash of brilliant blue-green (phthalocyanine green) is mixed for the bird's body, and laid on very lightly over the yellow to allow it to show through the green. Take care, however, not to lift it and cause it to become mixed with the green. The beak and eye are now put in with a medium grey and black.

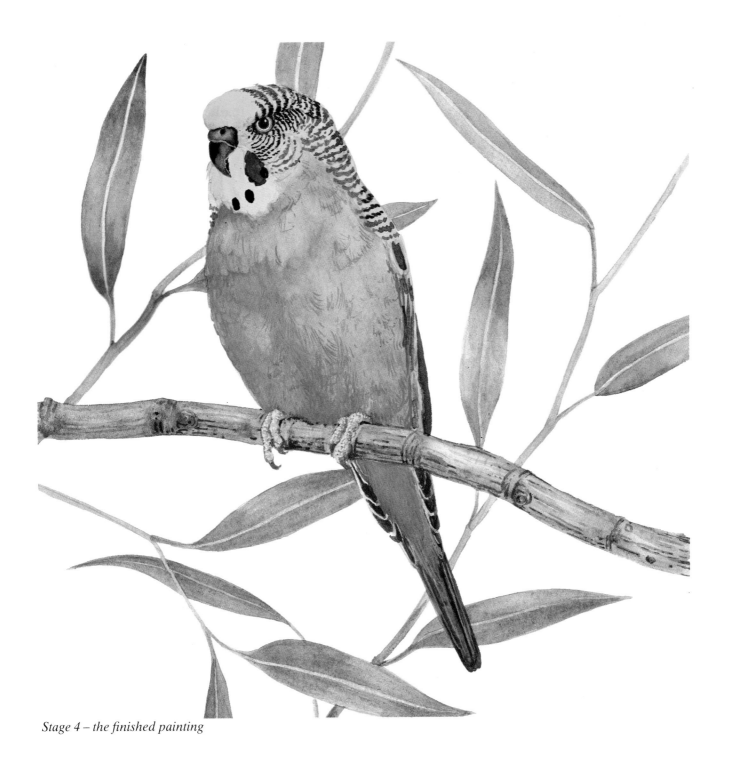

Stage 4 – the finished painting

Stage 4 – the finished painting

The black markings on the head, neck, wings and tail, and the details of texture on the branch, are now added.

A strong wash of manganese blue is put on to the tail, at its fullest intensity at the tip, and merging into the green where the tail meets the body.

Tropical fish

Original size: 358 × 530mm/14¼ × 21¼in.
Paper: Mould-made Whatman 300gsm/140lb.

This painting of an aquarium with tropical fish is an ambitious one, and one that cannot be hurried over. The lighting of the tank means that the background is varied in tone, some of the weeds being lit up brilliantly, while the thick growth of the weed throws large parts of the interior of the tank into deep shadow.

Care must be taken that the picture does not become so confused that the subjects (the fish) get lost among the variously lit elements of their setting. The fish, being shiny and iridescent and usually brightly coloured as well, are on the whole shown up best by a dark background; but if the entire interior of the tank is darkened, there is no source of light to account for the illumination of the fish; also the large area of dark background would make a less interesting picture. The way out of the difficulty seems to be to place most of the fish so that they have a background that enables them to show up – we can afford to have a few that are not well lit, in the interests of realism.

The individual fish are interestingly varied in shape and colour; some are brilliant, some strikingly patterned, some very delicately coloured, with markings that look faint at one moment and lit up with colour at the next. The scales of all the fish are of a silvery iridescence that comes and goes with each fish's movements.

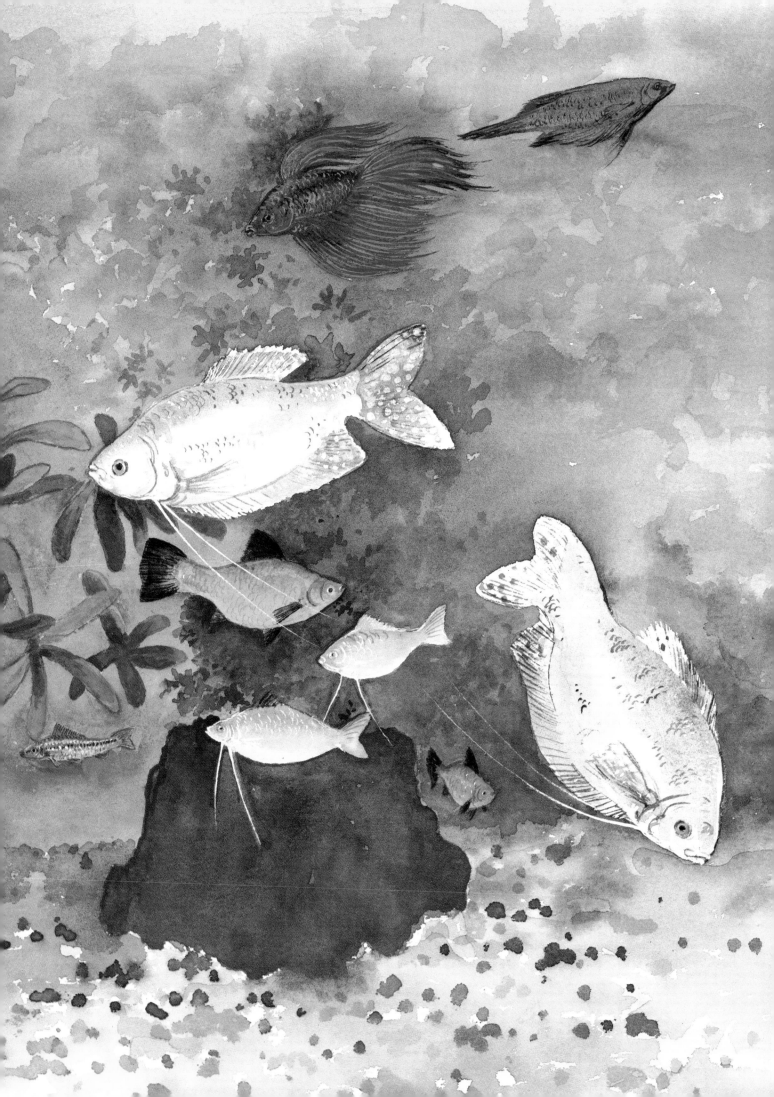

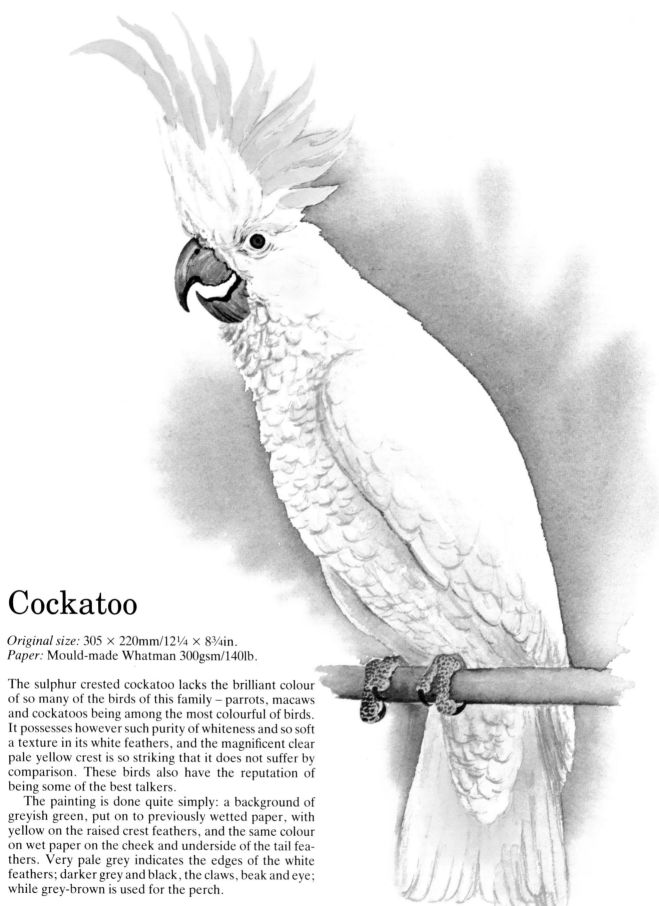

Cockatoo

Original size: 305 × 220mm/12¼ × 8¾in.
Paper: Mould-made Whatman 300gsm/140lb.

The sulphur crested cockatoo lacks the brilliant colour of so many of the birds of this family – parrots, macaws and cockatoos being among the most colourful of birds. It possesses however such purity of whiteness and so soft a texture in its white feathers, and the magnificent clear pale yellow crest is so striking that it does not suffer by comparison. These birds also have the reputation of being some of the best talkers.

The painting is done quite simply: a background of greyish green, put on to previously wetted paper, with yellow on the raised crest feathers, and the same colour on wet paper on the cheek and underside of the tail feathers. Very pale grey indicates the edges of the white feathers; darker grey and black, the claws, beak and eye; while grey-brown is used for the perch.

HORSES

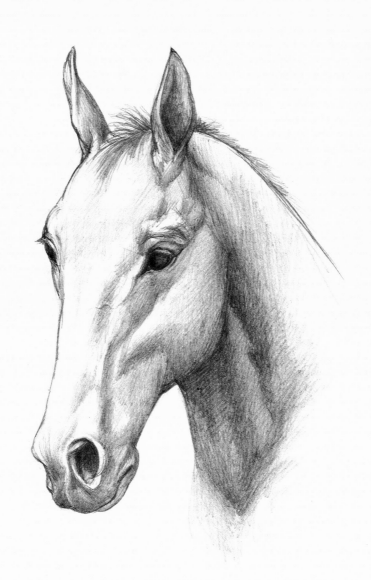

Drawing horses

The drawings on these two pages are characteristic of those which an animal painter is constantly making in the course of his work; when, as in this case, the purpose is to study how animals move, the number of separate drawings is higher than when one is working on a less mobile subject, and the degree of finish is deliberately not great. The drawings shown were done from a television broadcast of show-jumping at Hickstead, and they had to be done very quickly, in very short bursts, for the television presentation constantly changes its viewpoint; how often one longs for another second's view of a horse! But television is a great blessing, bringing into one's home so many sights that one might never otherwise see, and sometimes in the sort of close-up that would never be possible.

Only one of these drawings includes the rider, as the main purpose was to record the action of the horses.

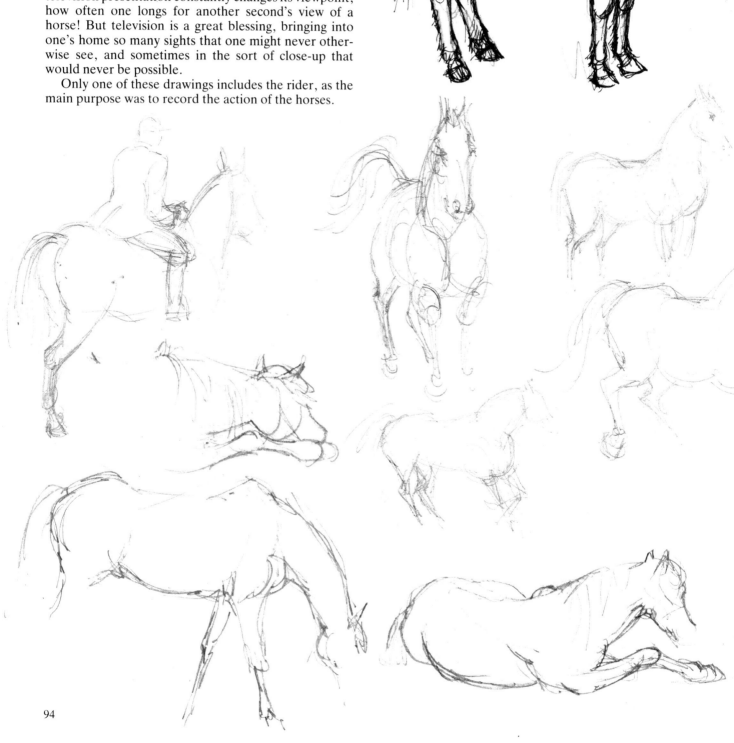

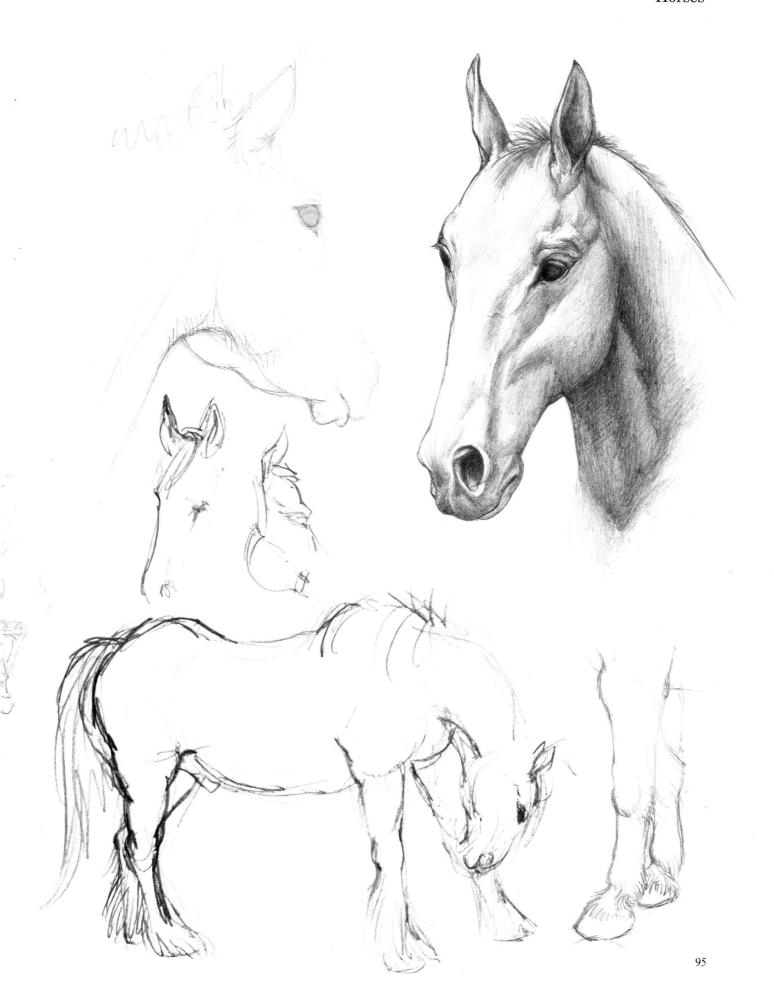

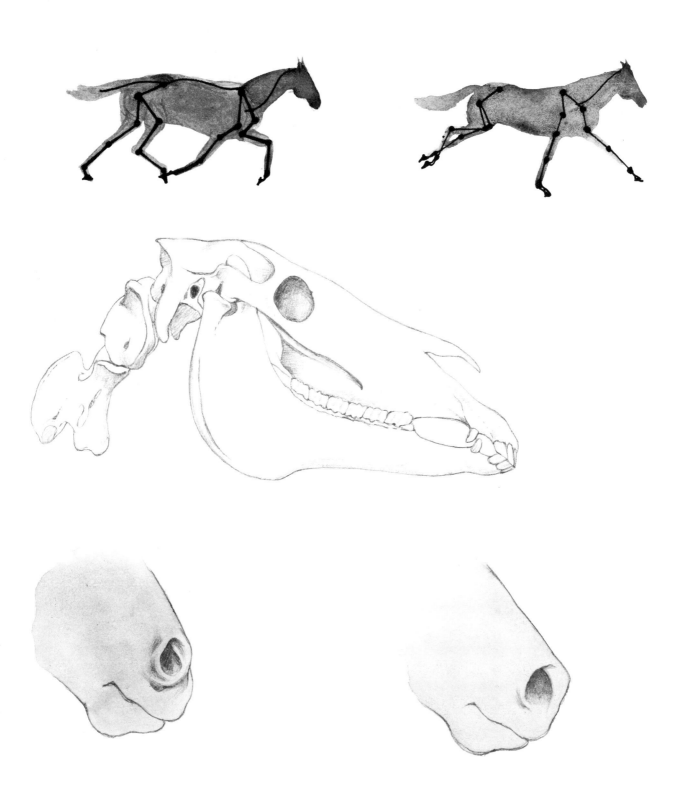

Anatomy of the horse

When you are drawing horses, a knowledge of their anatomy is of great assistance. For instance, when you draw a horse's head, it is remarkably easy to place the eye too low – with all hooved animals, the eye is rather high – in general, their heads have a large amount of face to a small amount of brain.

The drawing of the horse's skull (middle) shows the position of the eye very high up. The two drawings opposite demonstrate how the ear pivots and will sometimes appear to be forward and sometimes right behind the head.

The small figures of running horses, with lines showing how the legs articulate, illustrate another important point, namely the position of the forelegs, and the considerable distance between the leading leg and the trail-

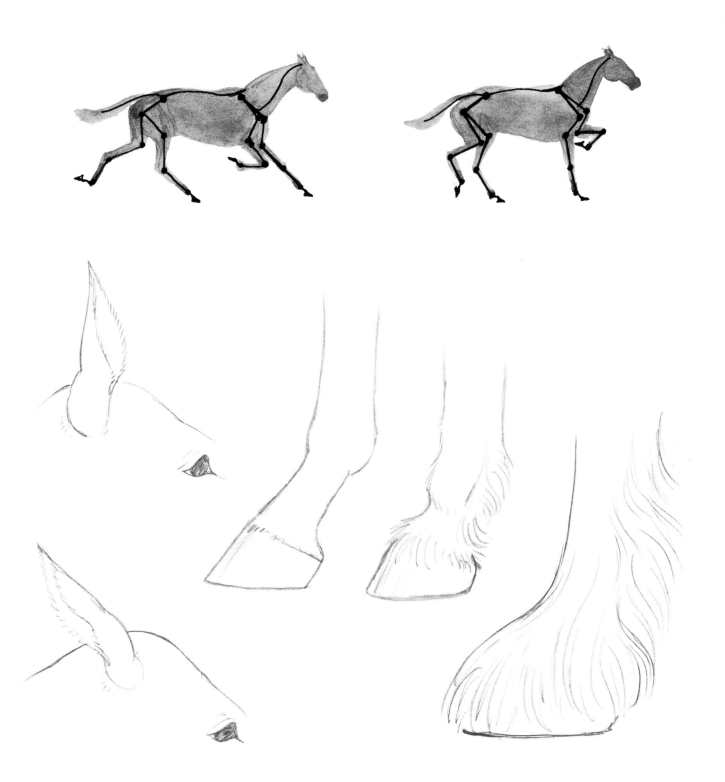

ing one, very widely separated where they emerge below the chest. The lines show how the forelegs pivot from a point at the very top of the body, that the bones of the leg itself move as one unit with the shoulder-blade, and that it is at the upper end of this bone that the movement originates.

The drawings at the bottom left-hand corner show a horse's nostril as it is in repose, and how it is greatly extended when the horse is exerting itself and breathing deeply. This completely changes, of course, the shape of

the animal's face, the end of the muzzle becoming almost square; and this change must be taken into account when you are drawing a running or jumping horse.

The three drawings of hooves show a comparison between the feet of different kinds of horse: first, the long slender sloping pastern of the thoroughbred, built for speed, which can be compared with the conformation of the feet of such dogs as greyhounds; secondly, the shorter more upright shape of the cob; and, third, the huge hairy foot of the shire horse.

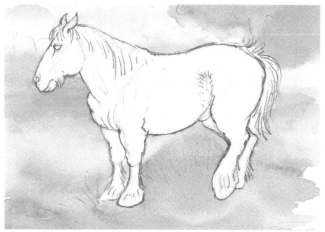

Stage 1

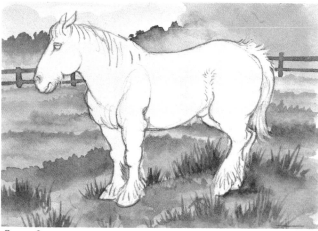

Stage 2

Heavy horse: demonstration

Original size: 160 × 225mm/6¼ × 9in.
Paper: Mould-made Whatman 300gsm/140lb.

The heavy horses – the Shire, Clydesdale, Suffolk Punch, and Percheron – have a special charm. Impressive in their massive strength and size, and endearingly gentle and good-tempered, they are now to some extent recovering from the drastic reduction in their numbers which followed the farming trade's rush to embrace mechanisation, and the swallowing up of so many small local breweries that kept a stable of these horses. Nevertheless some of the surviving large breweries have retained their heavy horses and contributed greatly to the revival of interest in them.

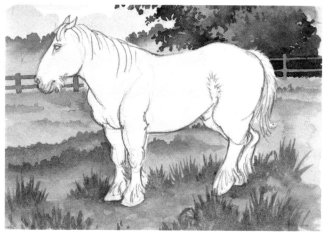

Stage 3

Stage 1

Having made a careful drawing of the horse, the background is dealt with before continuing on the animal. Some pale blue (cobalt) and grey clouds about the horizon (cobalt with a little burnt sienna) are washed in in very light tones; the field is also washed in, very pale, with yellow-green (lemon yellow, phthalocyanine blue, and a touch of burnt sienna) and pale yellow ochre, in irregular zones of colour; also, for the nearer trees, some yellow-green, a little bluer than the grass.

Stage 2

The distant trees (a more bluish green still) and the rough grass of the field (more burnt sienna in the green) are added at this stage, as well as the fence on the far side of the horse's field.

Stage 3

Now the nearer trees are finished with quite a dark brownish green, slightly blued here and there, and allowed to be darkest where they come behind the fence on the right.

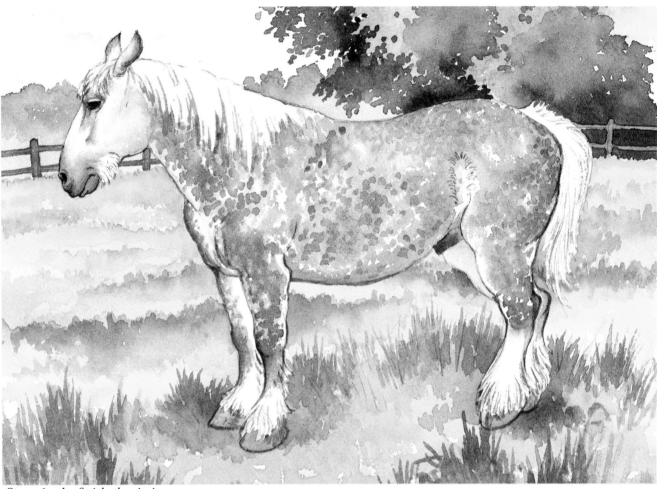

Stage 4 – the finished painting

Stage 4 – the finished painting

The horse now has its dappled pattern added, with a grey mixed from Payne's grey and burnt umber, put on so as to leave white spots, with darker grey spots dabbed on as the wash dries. Detail is added to sharpen the eye, nose, ears, mane and tail and the edges are strengthened. The hooves are finished in grey and yellow ochre.

Horse's head: demonstration

Original size: 225mm sq./9in. sq.
Paper: Mould-made Whatman 180gsm/90lb.

I have chosen a direct profile view of the head of a thoroughbred for this demonstration; and I have used a method rather different from the other ones in this book. This is to do an underpainting in monochrome, with the colour put on in a separate operation.

As usual, the first stage is that of extremely careful drawing. The horse, as the subject of a painting, is one which easily attracts criticism because of horse lovers' tendency to find imperfections in the picture rather than in the model. So when you embark on your picture, you must decide whether you want to paint an idealisation of the breed, or the portrait of an individual animal. My own taste is for the portrait, 'warts and all', but the alternative is perfectly acceptable, and to achieve it, one must study many different animals which are regarded as possessing the required qualities. Photographs are of great use here, as measurements can be made, and one compared with another. When you do this, take care to allow for distortions of dimensions due to the position of the camera in relation to the model; look carefully, and assess whether it was level, high or low, from behind or in front, or an absolute profile. Knowledge of anatomy is useful here, to analyse the information which photographs convey.

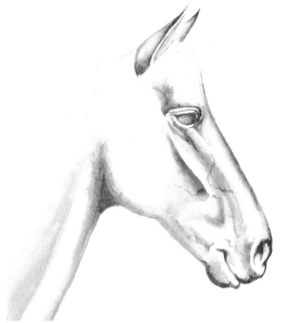

Stage 1

Stage 1

The drawing is transferred to the chosen paper; then, with a wash of a brown mixed from burnt umber and ultramarine, a careful monochrome wash drawing of the form is built up. This tone is applied only where it is necessary to darken the overall colour – the light parts are left untouched.

Stage 2

The background colour is put on, and the tone varied by darkening the ultramarine/Payne's grey wash with additional grey.

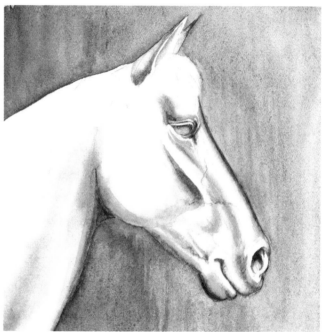

Stage 2

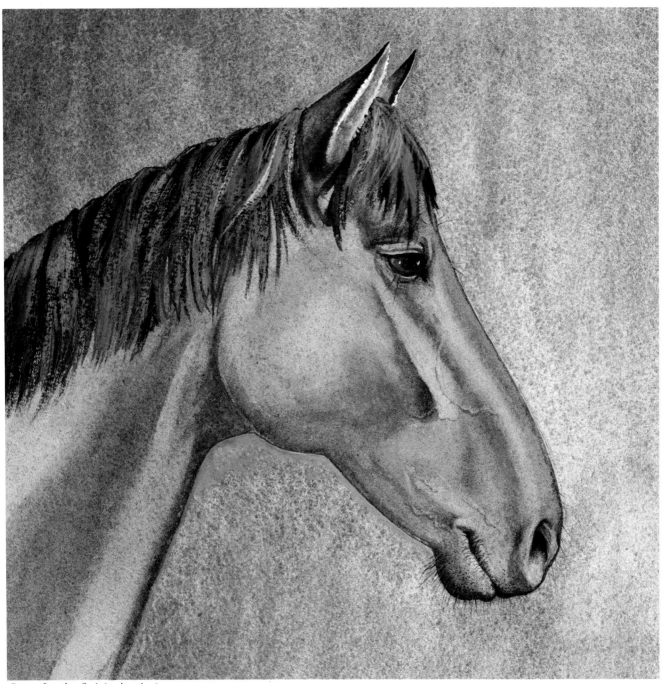

Stage 3 – the finished painting

Stage 3 – the finished painting

The whole is now left to dry thoroughly – this is where a hairdryer can be very useful – but do not start using it too soon, or you may get unwanted hard edges; however it can be very useful when the paper is generally damp without any actually wet patches.

The colour of the horse's hair is mixed (in this case, burnt sienna with a little yellow ochre) in a fairly thin wash, and applied quickly over the whole head. When this is dry, the eye, mane, and the sharp details around the nostril and mouth, and odd hairs are added with a stronger black. A little opaque white is used to mix a grey to highlight the mane.

Shire horse

The shire horse on this page, and the thoroughbred mare with her foal opposite, show how these two types of horse differ. The shire, which sometimes weighs as much as a ton, and has the legs necessary to support this weight as well as an enormously strong physique, can pull a weight of five tons; it is probably the descendant of the great horses which used to carry men-in-armour.

The painting is carried out in a very sketchy washy style, with details kept to a minimum.

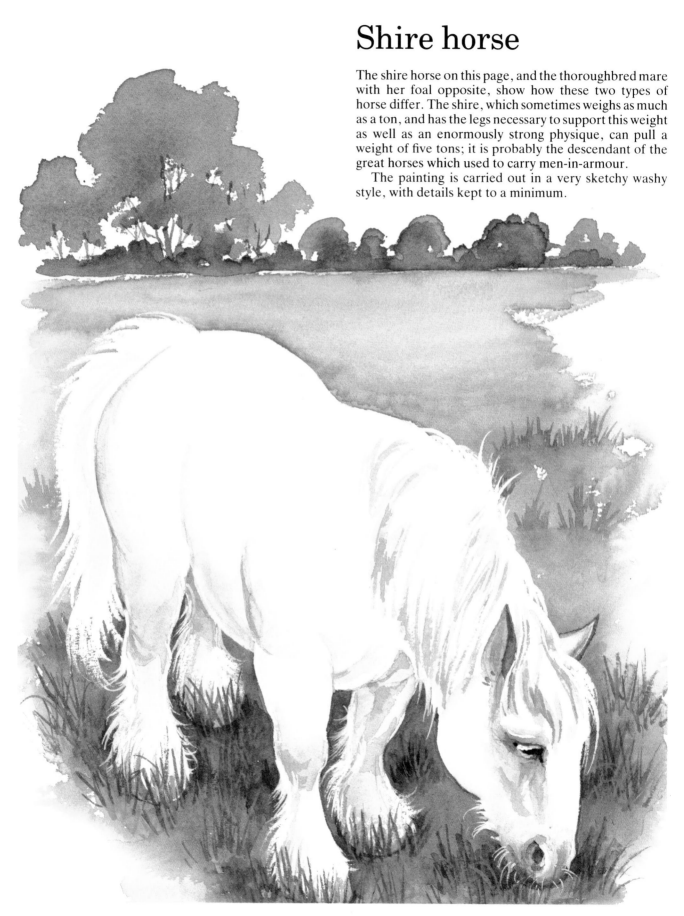

Thoroughbred

The thoroughbred, of course, is bred for speed, with long legs, slender build, and refined appearance. The huge industry that has been built up around it – flat racing, breeding and training, let alone betting – involves vast amounts of money and people, yet it all started with three horses: the Darley Arabian, the Godolphin Arabian, and the Byerley Turk.

The picture is executed with a fairly free, washy technique. The animals have been drawn with a brush line in black. The grassy background is little more than a plain wash of yellow-green, with tufts of grass drawn in dark green with a size 1 brush, except where dark green has been washed over the ground beneath the mare; here the grass is drawn in a very pale opaque green.

The glossy smooth coats are painted with free broad brush strokes of varying tones of brown, with strong and weak black washes for manes, tails, noses, and legs.

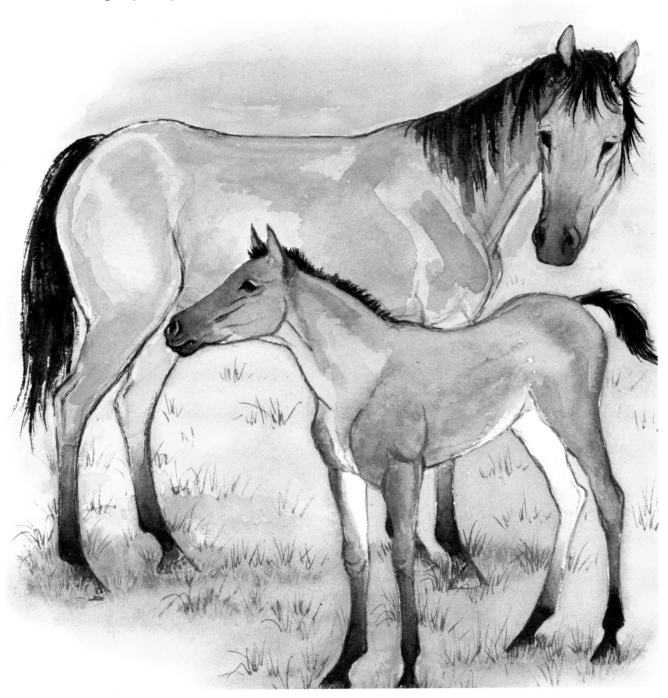

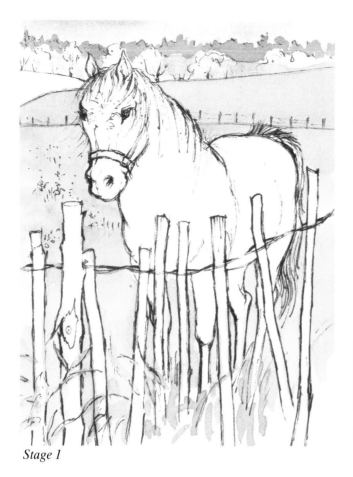

Stage 1

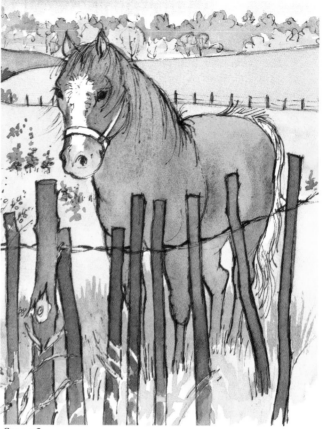

Stage 2

Horse looking over a fence: demonstration

Original size: 290 × 222mm/11½ × 8¾in.
Paper: Mould-made Whatman 180gsm/90lb.

Stage 1

The first stage is a pen drawing of the horse; the position and size of the animal had previously been roughed out on the Whatman paper used for the painting, and the pen drawing done directly from life. Washes were applied of Payne's grey on the sky, and pale yellow-green on the field in the foreground; a little burnt sienna was added to the green for the embankment, and grey for the distant hill; a darker blue-grey green was used for the distant trees. Yellow ochre and a lemon-yellow-green mixture are added on the horse's field.

Stage 2

Patches of yellow, orange and sharp lemon are put on the trees in the middle distance; Winsor violet and burnt sienna on the ploughed field, and dark green on the small trees on the left. The fence posts are put in with a green/brown/grey mixture, and some darker blue-green round the horse's feet. A pale wash of pink is put on the nose, then a wash of burnt sienna over the body, leaving the white blaze untouched, and blending with the tone on the nose. More burnt sienna is used for the dead dock plants.

Stage 3 – the finished painting

The horse is completed with black on nose, tail, mane and feet. Ultramarine and Payne's grey are mixed for the bridle, and much dark green detail on the grass in the foreground, and on the piece of hedge-plant on the left, completes the picture.

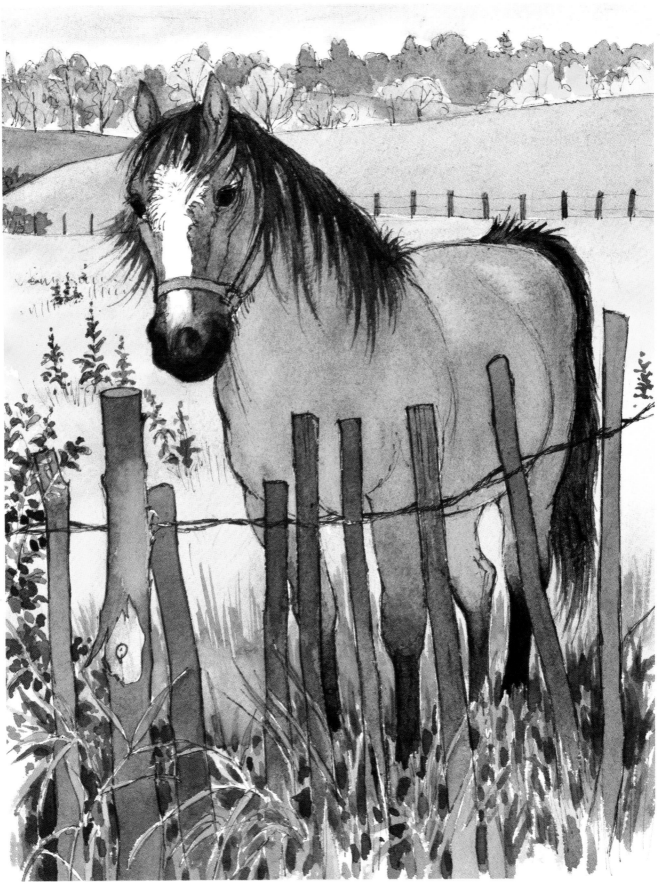

Stage 3 – the finished painting

Horses in a paddock

Original size: 358 × 530mm/14¼ × 21¼in.
Paper: Mould-made Saunders Not 300gsm/140lb.

This scene is based on one of a kind still often seen in the countryside; a peaceful scene of a number of assorted horses and ponies in a large field, with a background of trees and farm buildings. The picture, which is painted with a fairly free, loose treatment, features the varied greens of early summer. Masking solution has been used for the fence, the white horse and the blossom.

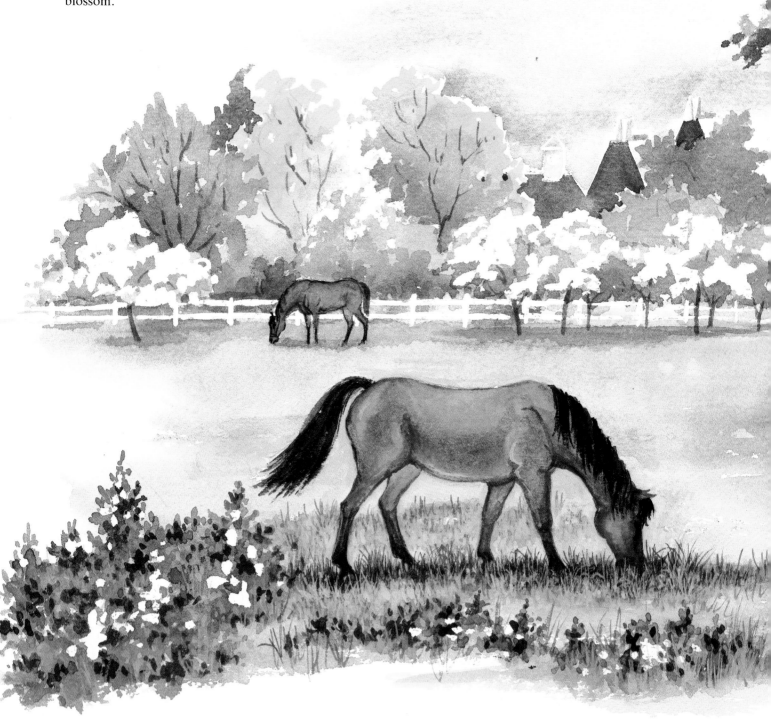

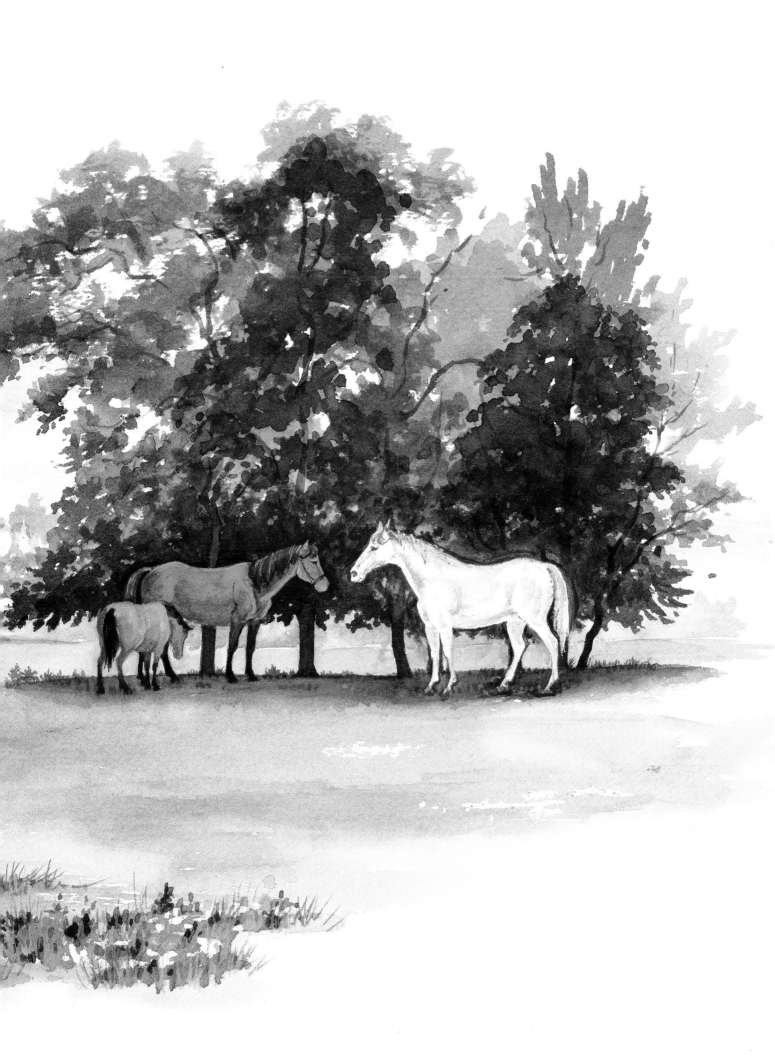

Donkeys

Original size: 200 × 210mm/8 × 8½in.
Paper: Mould-made Saunders 180gsm/90lb.

These two young donkeys, in a field at a Kent National Trust site, seem to be seeking the company of human visitors, since they spend most of their time at the side of the field where the public footpath runs. I had plenty of time, therefore, to make this drawing of them. They are fairly dark in colour, but donkeys often are much lighter, with longer, shaggier coats.

The colour used was a mixture of burnt sienna, lamp black, and Winsor violet, washed on over the whole bodies with the tone varied by thinning out the colour or by adding more pigment.

A very light yellow-green is used as a basic wash for the grass, and the clumps of grass are indicated with a darker, olive, green, mixed from lemon cadmium and black. Finally, the dark details are added, and a few light hairs on noses and ears put on with opaque white with a little of the purple-grey mixed in.

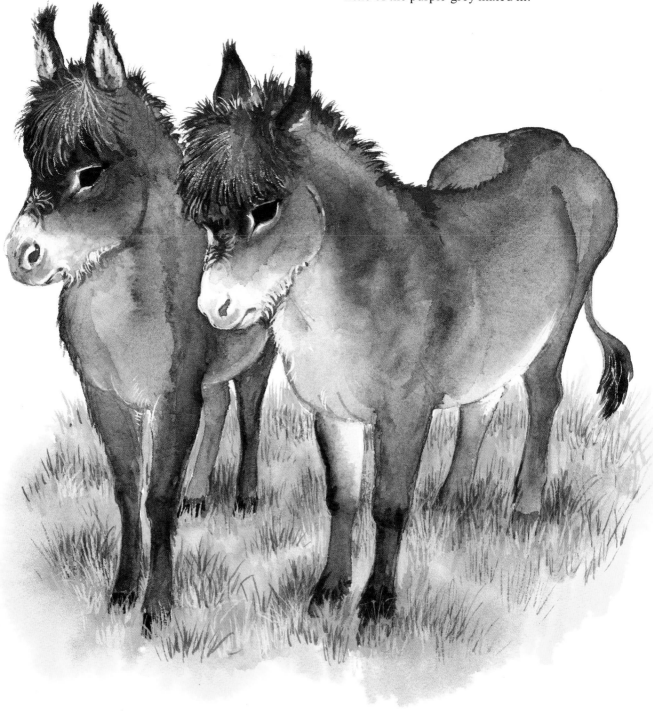

ANIMALS IN GARDENS, PARKS, AND FIELDS

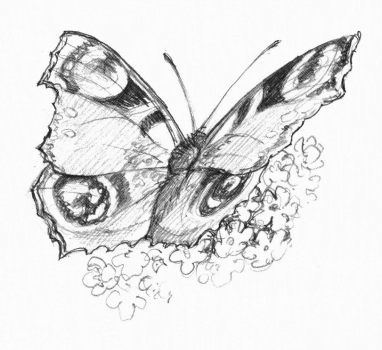

Animals in gardens, parks and fields

Apart from portraying the animals that we live with, there are many other ways of increasing the scope of one's animal work and interests.

People who live in large cities, particularly those in flats, may find it impractical to keep pets of their own, but parks and large gardens supply some contact with, or at least sight of animals. Fallow and other kinds of deer are to be found in many large parks; for example the black fallow deer of Epping Forest are well known, and in different parts of the country the variety is greater and more exotic. Woburn Park has many kinds of hoofed mammals, including American bison such as the one illustrated on page 109.

All the parks are full of small birds, and most have grey squirrels. These are often exceedingly tame, and will take food from the hands of visitors. This is of enormous help to the eager artist, who can take advantage of the activities of other people, or himself bribe the squirrels to stay and be drawn.

Apart from these opportunities, if one comes across animals by the roadside which have been killed by traffic but not too badly damaged, these can be invaluable, as through them one can really discover the exact structure of feet, ears, fur growth patterns and other such details, and make measured drawings. Draw the head, or limbs, from different viewpoints; and use these studies in conjunction with your drawings from the living animal. They will help you to make a really well observed and thoroughly worked out painting. Some drawings of these kinds are shown here; and some of this type of material was used for the grey squirrel demonstration painting overleaf.

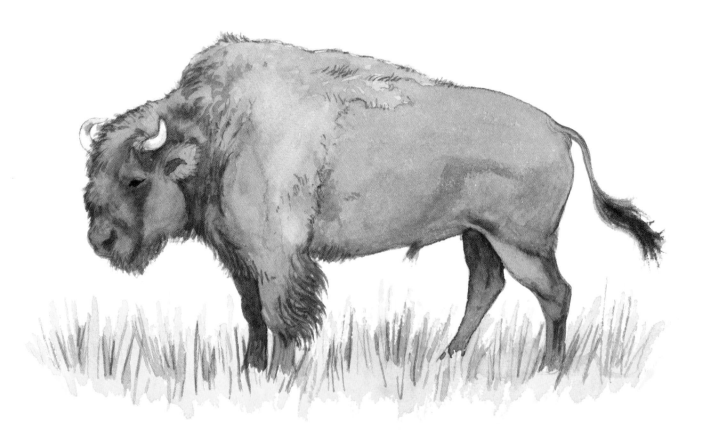

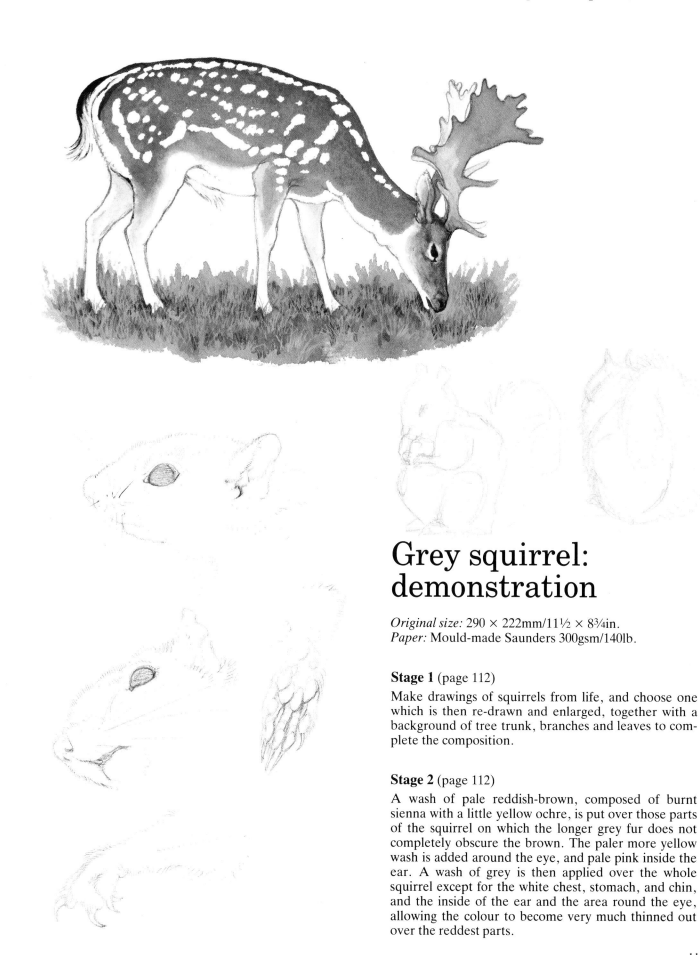

Grey squirrel: demonstration

Original size: 290 × 222mm/11½ × 8¾in.
Paper: Mould-made Saunders 300gsm/140lb.

Stage 1 (page 112)

Make drawings of squirrels from life, and choose one which is then re-drawn and enlarged, together with a background of tree trunk, branches and leaves to complete the composition.

Stage 2 (page 112)

A wash of pale reddish-brown, composed of burnt sienna with a little yellow ochre, is put over those parts of the squirrel on which the longer grey fur does not completely obscure the brown. The paler more yellow wash is added around the eye, and pale pink inside the ear. A wash of grey is then applied over the whole squirrel except for the white chest, stomach, and chin, and the inside of the ear and the area round the eye, allowing the colour to become very much thinned out over the reddest parts.

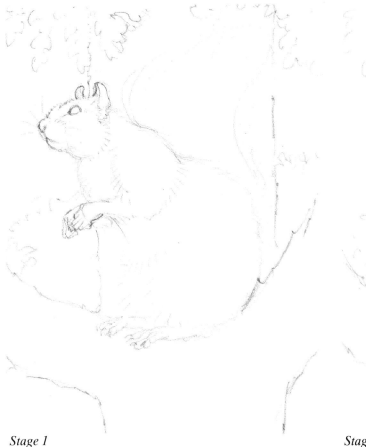

Stage 1

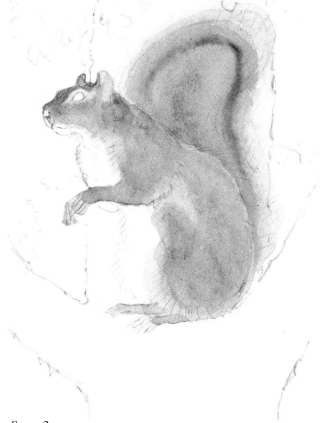

Stage 2

Stage 3

A very pale cobalt blue wash is put on the sky, yellow-green on the trees in the background, and deeper green on the leaves above the squirrel. These washes of green should not be flat, but should have variations of colour and tone – yellowish, and bluer, deeper tones are used to give variety and form without going into much detail.

A dark brown wash is applied over the trunk and limbs of the tree – a mixture of burnt sienna, black and a little violet. When this wash is half-dry, a very strong mixture of the same colour is used to define the texture of the bark and the edges of the leaves at the top. The squirrel's eye is added in black; just before it is dry, water is dropped into the middle and blotted up with a squeezed out brush.

Stage 4 – the finished painting (page 113)

The ears, toes, claws, and nose are next defined with a fine brush, and many hairs added: long ones on the tail; first black and very dark grey over the central part; then white ones, mainly around the edges, a few over the central part. These long white hairs form a diffuse outer zone all over the tail, but the reddish colour shows through, and through the similar layer of black hairs which underlie the white.

Short hairs are put in on the squirrel's body, head and feet, and the whiskers finish the painting.

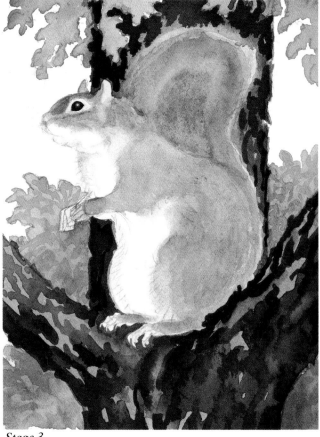

Stage 3

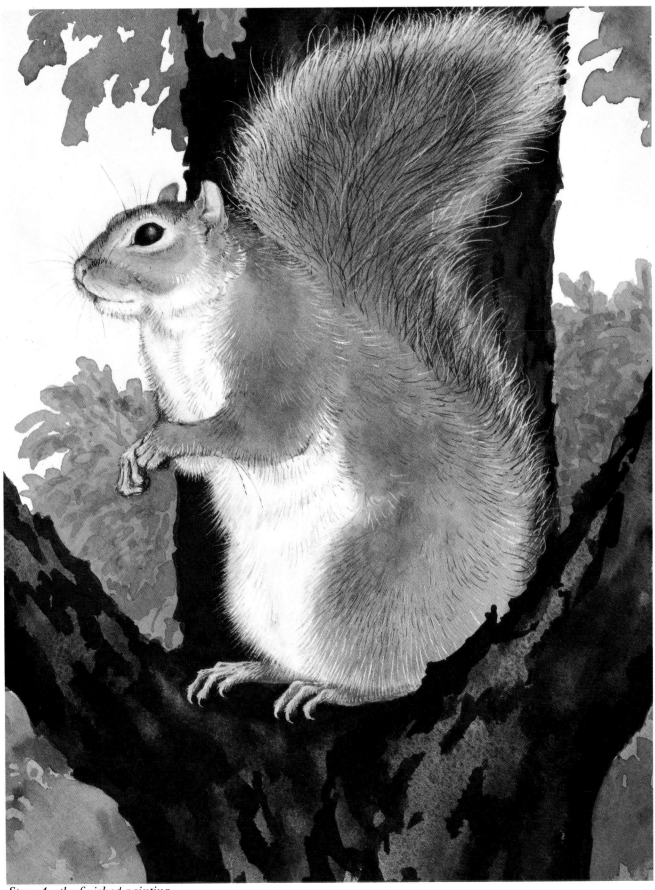

Stage 4 – the finished painting

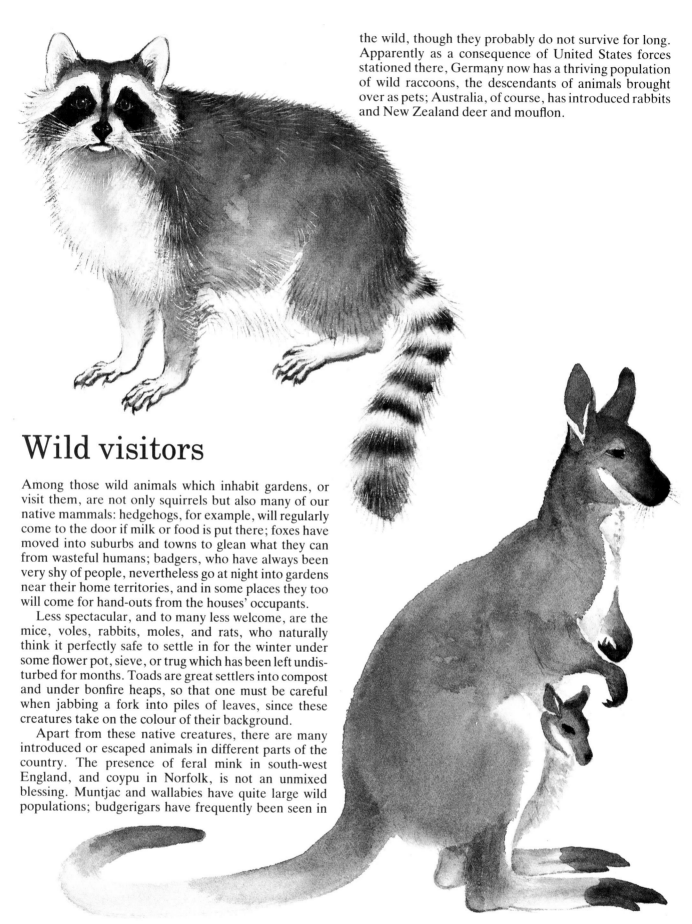

the wild, though they probably do not survive for long. Apparently as a consequence of United States forces stationed there, Germany now has a thriving population of wild raccoons, the descendants of animals brought over as pets; Australia, of course, has introduced rabbits and New Zealand deer and mouflon.

Wild visitors

Among those wild animals which inhabit gardens, or visit them, are not only squirrels but also many of our native mammals: hedgehogs, for example, will regularly come to the door if milk or food is put there; foxes have moved into suburbs and towns to glean what they can from wasteful humans; badgers, who have always been very shy of people, nevertheless go at night into gardens near their home territories, and in some places they too will come for hand-outs from the houses' occupants.

Less spectacular, and to many less welcome, are the mice, voles, rabbits, moles, and rats, who naturally think it perfectly safe to settle in for the winter under some flower pot, sieve, or trug which has been left undisturbed for months. Toads are great settlers into compost and under bonfire heaps, so that one must be careful when jabbing a fork into piles of leaves, since these creatures take on the colour of their background.

Apart from these native creatures, there are many introduced or escaped animals in different parts of the country. The presence of feral mink in south-west England, and coypu in Norfolk, is not an unmixed blessing. Muntjac and wallabies have quite large wild populations; budgerigars have frequently been seen in

The animals illustrated here have been portrayed in varying ways; the *hedgehogs* are painted with a wash of yellow ochre/Payne's grey/burnt sienna for the head, feet and lower part of the body; the prickles are put in with individual brush strokes for each, the colour varied to convey the mixture of grey brown and white on each spine.

The *fox cub* is given a pale red-brown wet wash, largely burnt sienna, with black washed over on paws, face and ear, partly while the first wash was still damp, and built up further as it dried. Hairs, eyes, nose, and the edges of some parts were then drawn on with a fine brush using whatever colour was called for, from black to light brown. Both of these paintings were done on a fairly smooth not-pressed Saunders paper.

A much heavier mould-made Whatman Rough was used for the *raccoon* and the *wallaby*, which shows in the greater degree of texture in the wash. The raccoon was handled similarly to the fox cub, with the addition of opaque white hairs applied over darker wash.

The *wallaby* and *joey* were painted almost entirely with a wet wash, with burnt sienna mixed with yellow ochre, and thin lamp-black washed into the wet ground where required. The brown on the toes of the hind feet, the eyes and inside of the ears, and the noses and whiskers were added after the wash was dry, but the fine details were kept to an absolute minimum, and the character of the paper allowed to play a major part in the picture.

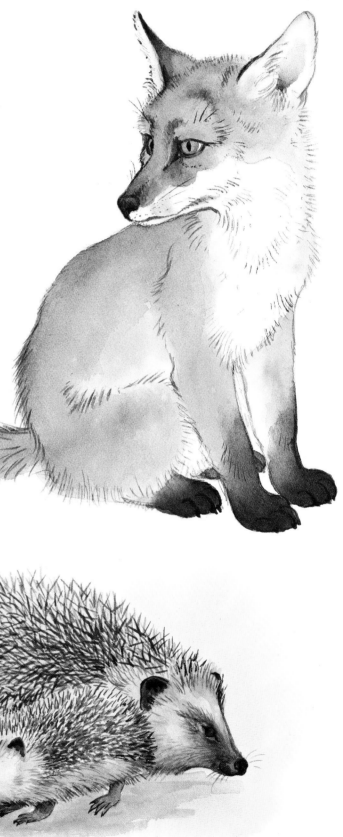

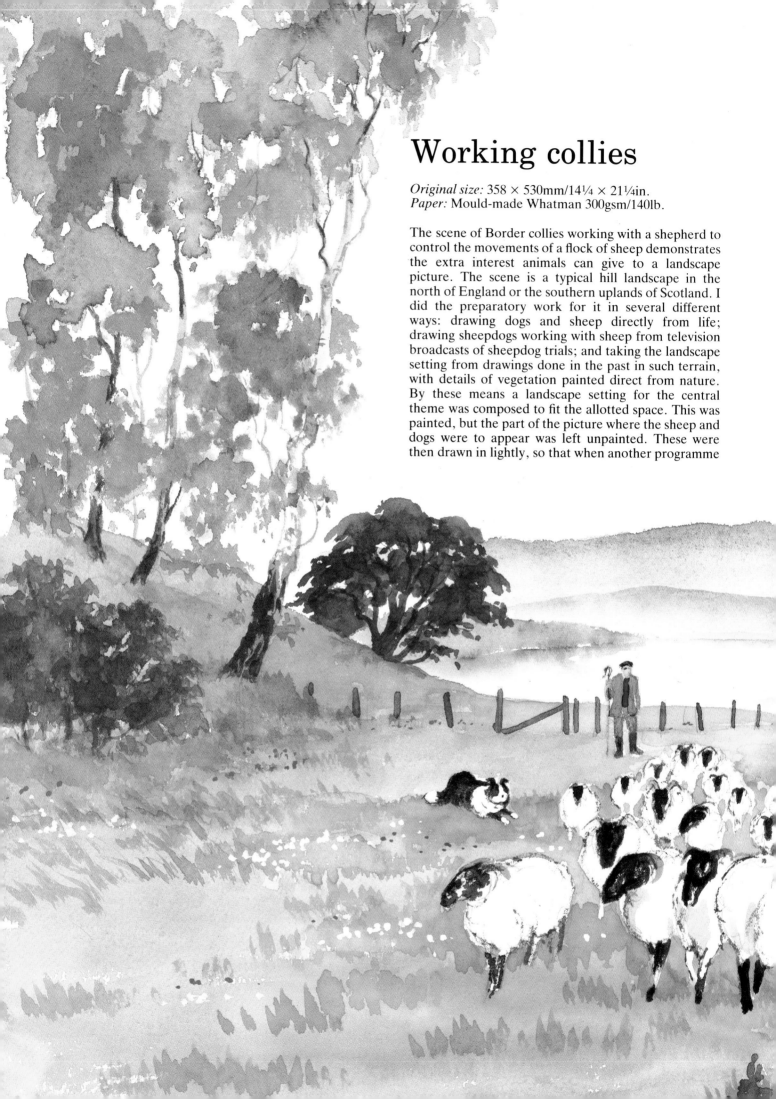

Working collies

Original size: 358 × 530mm/14¼ × 21¼in.
Paper: Mould-made Whatman 300gsm/140lb.

The scene of Border collies working with a shepherd to control the movements of a flock of sheep demonstrates the extra interest animals can give to a landscape picture. The scene is a typical hill landscape in the north of England or the southern uplands of Scotland. I did the preparatory work for it in several different ways: drawing dogs and sheep directly from life; drawing sheepdogs working with sheep from television broadcasts of sheepdog trials; and taking the landscape setting from drawings done in the past in such terrain, with details of vegetation painted direct from nature. By these means a landscape setting for the central theme was composed to fit the allotted space. This was painted, but the part of the picture where the sheep and dogs were to appear was left unpainted. These were then drawn in lightly, so that when another programme of sheepdog trials was due, I was able to make the final drawing of all the figures, in effect, from life, though of necessity very quickly. But a great deal of the preliminary work had been done, although only two dogs were used from the dozen sheets I had previously filled with sketches and drawings of sheep, dogs and shepherds.

The animals were then finished, and the foreground of grass, the dried spikes of dock plants, the marguerites and poppies completed to round off the whole composition.

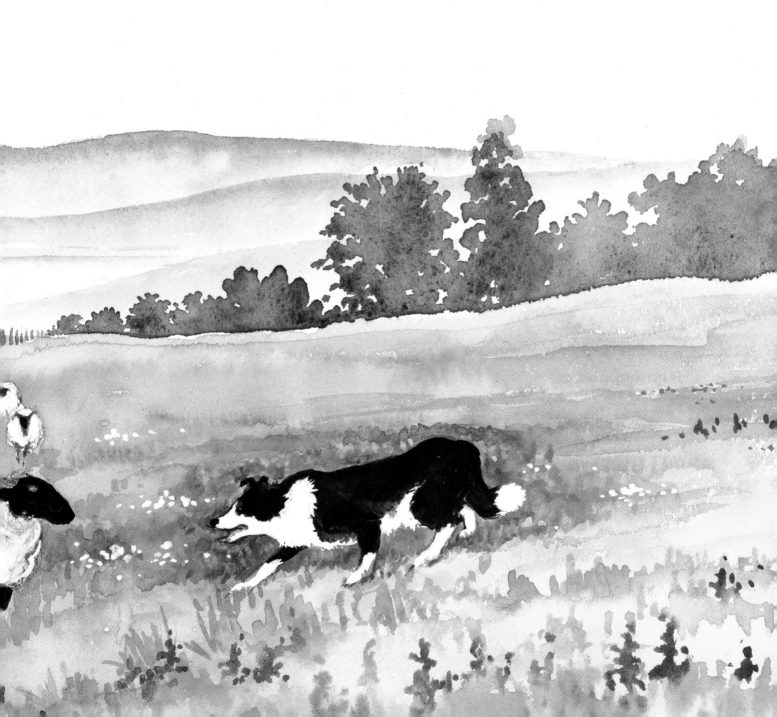

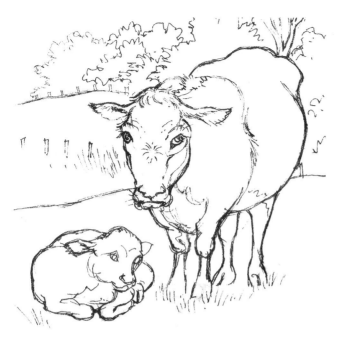

Stage 1

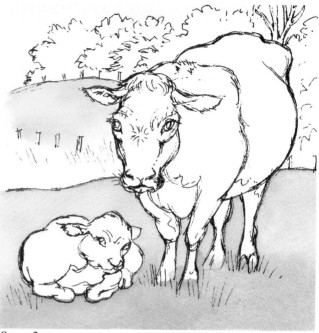

Stage 2

Cow and calf: demonstration

Original size: 225mm sq./9in. sq.
Paper: Mould-made Whatman 180gsm/90lb.

Unlike most of the other pictures in this book, the cow and its calf are painted in a combination of pen drawing and watercolour.

Stage 1

For the drawing I use a fairly coarse (0.6mm) Rötring pen, which takes waterproof black ink, as is, of course, necessary when it is combined with watercolour. On mould-made Whatman Rough paper, even this rather coarse pen makes a variable, not very thick, even slightly broken line, although where a solid line is needed it is achieved by working slowly.

Heavier drawing is reserved for the animals; but the line kept light in the background.

Stage 2

The foundation of the background is laid in pale washes: very pale cobalt for the sky; cadmium yellow merging with yellow ochre for the cornfield; and pale green, with a tinge of yellow ochre at the far edge for the foreground field, getting deeper and bluer where it reaches the animals' level. I use a mixture of pthalo-cyanine blue, cadmium yellow and a little burnt sienna to mix the green.

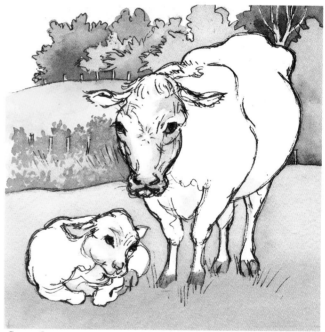

Stage 3

Stage 3

The trees beyond the cornfield are washed in, with varying greens, mixed from the same pigments in different proportions; the bank of nettles between the two fields is done in the same way. A pale yellow-grey (yellow ochre and black in a very weak mixture) is used for definition on the white parts of the cattle; the same, a little deeper, for the hooves; the eyes, noses and the inside of the calf's ear are also done at this stage, and the light brown fence posts too.

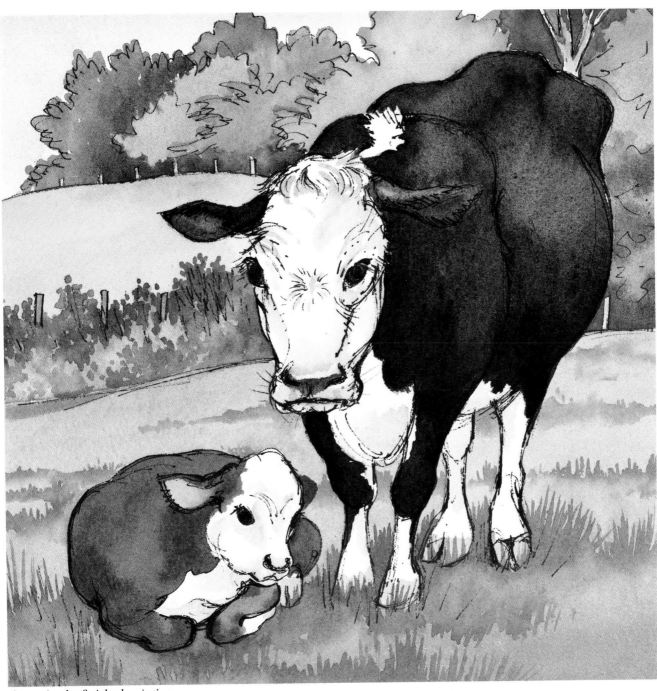

Stage 4 – the finished painting

Stage 4 – the finished painting

The coloured parts of the calf are added in a strong wash of burnt sienna, varying the tone to define the form. The black parts of the cow are painted next in the same fashion. By the time this is done, the calf is dry enough for me to put in some extra, deeper toned, detail on the grass around it, in a green with rather more burnt sienna in it. Some softer-edged lines of grass were then added on the further part of the field, with a slightly thinner wash of the same green.

Goats grazing

Original size: 290 × 500mm/11½ × 20in.
Paper: Mould-made Whatman 300gsm/140lb.

For the sake of the colour-balance of this scene of goats grazing it was fortunate that the nannies are Toggenburgs, and that the thistles they were eating at the time were in bloom. This lent itself to a pleasant, gentle colour scheme of soft greens, pale purple, and a nicely toning purple brown, while the picture shows that a composition can be satisfactorily carried out with only a restricted range of colour.

The goats were drawn as they fed, and I made many separate studies. It was necessary to follow them around and through the thistles, as they moved constantly and disappeared among the taller thistles as I worked. From the resulting sheaf of drawings, enough were selected to make up a balanced group, and drawn in position. The thistles are if anything slightly underdone; they were thick and abundant enough in reality to obscure the goats, so I was rather selective when it came to com-

posing the picture, preferring the main theme to be the goats rather than their food.

I used a fairly free treatment, painting one goat at a time, with a purplish brown mixed with Winsor violet and burnt sienna. First I wetted the paper round them, in order to apply a rather misty patch of pale green alternating with darker green to convey the rough character of the ground around the two animals on the left of the picture. The pale purplish thistles (Winsor violet with a little Permanent Rose) were added where I felt the composition demanded that colour; the diagonal patch from the top right corner forms a link between the separate groups of goats, connecting the small one at the back on the right with the two at the left of the picture, going right down to the left foreground, and then sweeping to

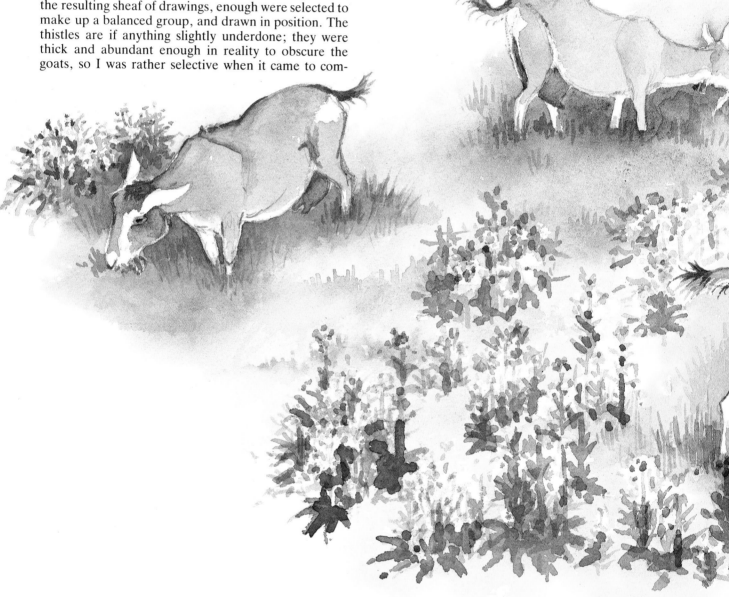

the right and enclosing the two nearest animals. The clump of flowers on the extreme left balances its counterpart at the right-hand side of the picture. When this was established, I completed the thistles with a darker, bluer green for the foliage, and strengthened the darker parts of the grass to give weight around the two large goats in the right foreground.

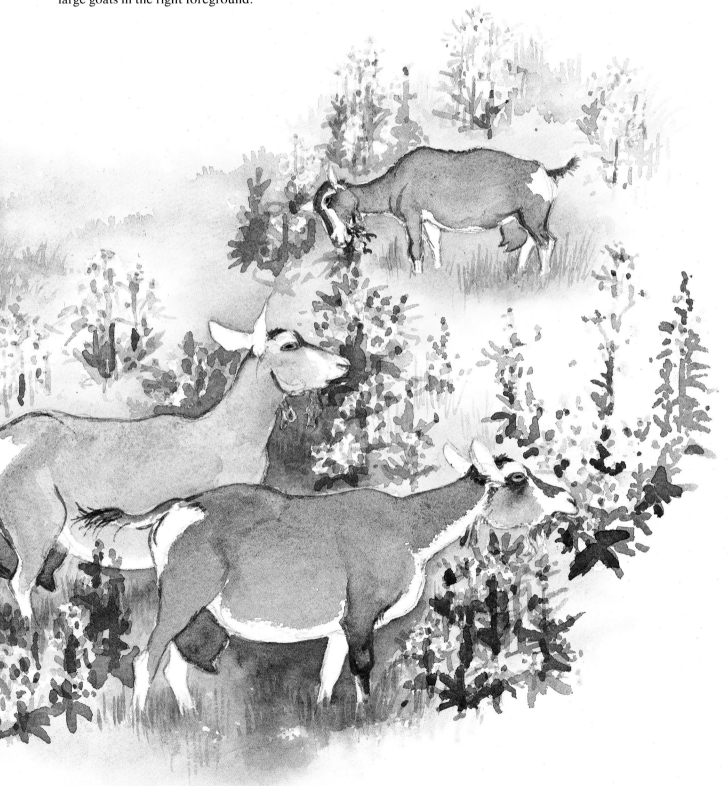

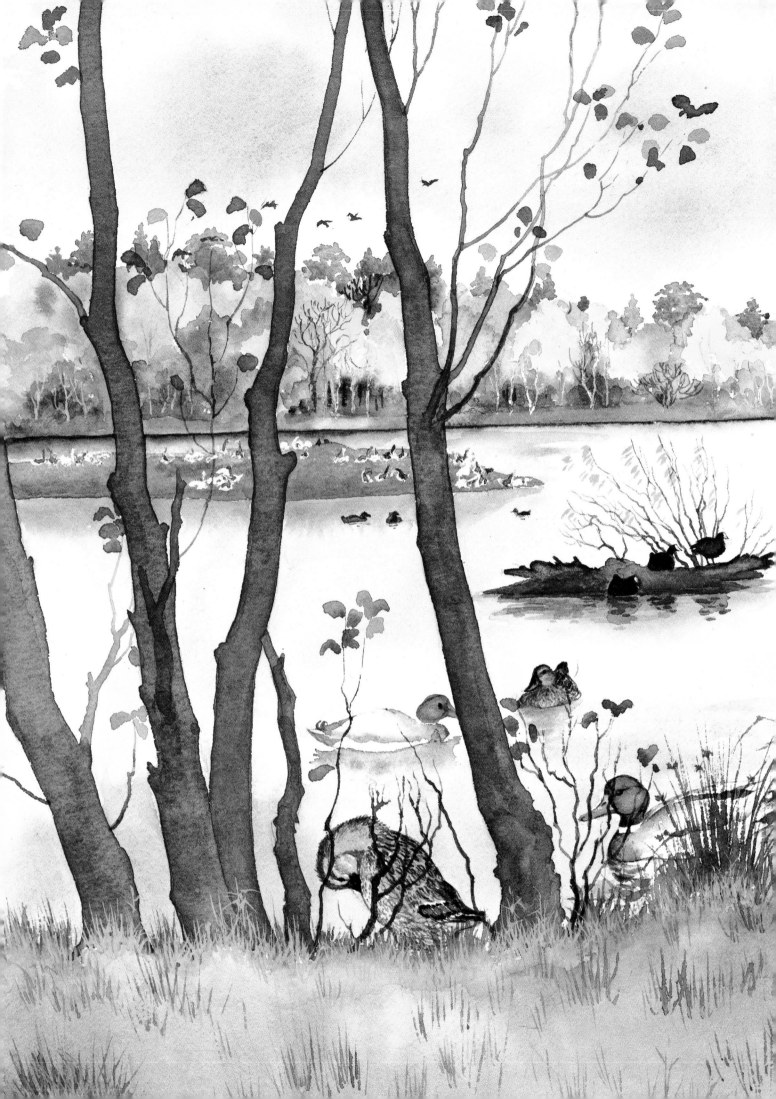

Waterfowl on a lake

Original size: 358 × 530mm/14¼ × 21¼in.
Paper: Mould-made Whatman 300gsm/140lb.

The painting of different kinds of waterfowl on a lake is the result of bringing together the product of several separate operations.

Three main elements go to make up this picture; a suitable setting for the subject; the lifelike presentation of wild or only semi-domestic birds, in the groupings and positions that they assume in such a setting; and, in order to give the birds sufficient prominence for them to be the subject of the picture, rather than details in a landscape, views of some of the birds from sufficiently near to show a degree of detail of colouring, pattern and conformation.

The setting is painted from studies of former gravel pits which have filled with water and provided a magnificent reserve for many species of birds; the place is so extensive that details have been moved together to provide a more compact background, retaining the vivid and varied autumn colours. The groupings of the flocks of birds are also seen in the waterfowl reserve, most of them too far off for detailed study. The birds in the foreground – the mallard and Chinese geese – are drawn and studied from close quarters in an urban park; care must be taken when transferring them to the wilder setting to place them so that they are the right size to fit into it naturally.

Masking fluid has been used on the swans, the rear parts of the geese, and the distant birds.

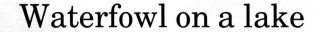

Bird table and garden

Original size: 358 × 530mm/14¼ × 21¼in.
Paper: Mould-made Whatman 300gsm/140lb.

Perhaps the most numerous and most easily observed of all the wild creatures that live in our gardens and streets are the garden birds that can be attracted to bird tables and windowsills. They are of course nervous and easily scared, but they can be watched from inside a room, so long as one stands hidden by a curtain, or far enough inside the room to be able to work without one's movements being seen. It is useful to keep a drawing board, paper and pencil always ready so that when birds come to the bird table you can start drawing them immediately. Do not be discouraged if it seems difficult; it is amazing how rapidly it becomes easier as knowledge increases and one becomes familiar with more species of birds. Such drawings can then be used to compose a comparatively large and complicated picture, such as the one on these two pages.

The wall and border of flowers and shrubs are designed to provide a colourful backdrop for the main theme of the picture – the bird table, with its water-dish, string of nuts and half-coconut, and the different kinds of bird on it and around it. The area of grass has been left deliberately featureless to provide a background for the small figures of the birds which would not compete with or obscure them.

The dark cypresses at the right-hand rear of the picture are similarly treated to provide a kind of enclosing end to the picture, as the left-hand end of the flower border does for its other side, and to balance the dark green of the white rose bush on the left.

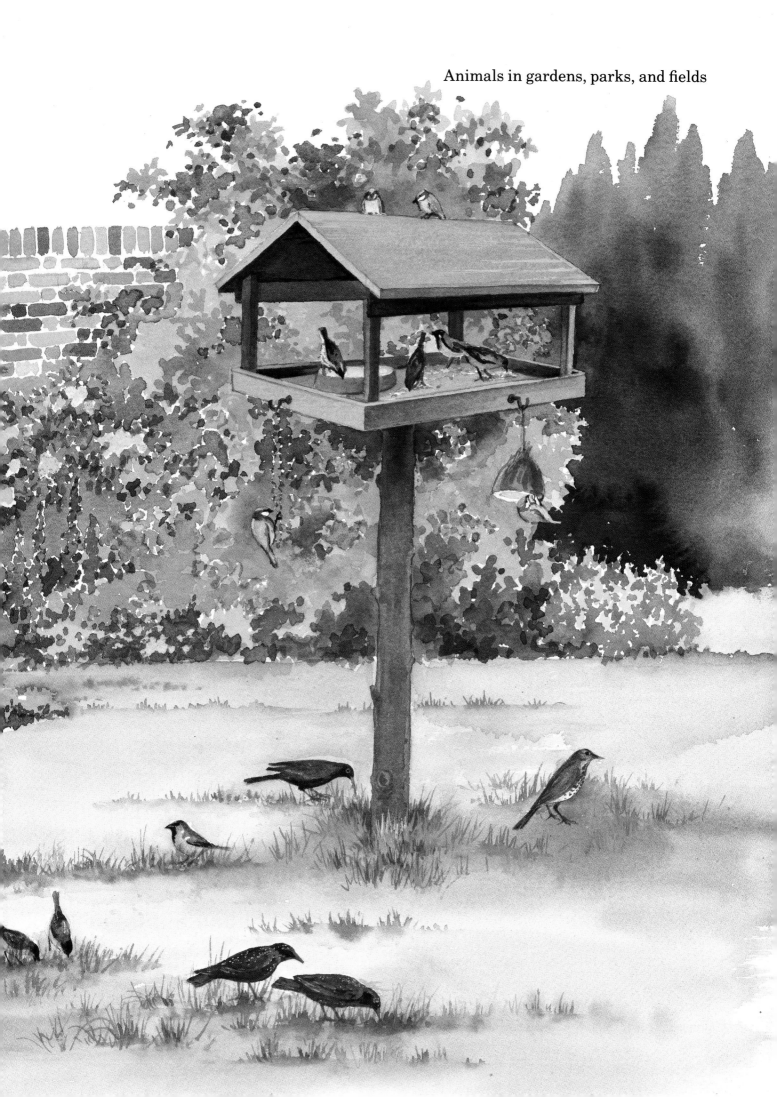

Animal portraits

Now that we have come to the last page of the book, I hope that what I have written and demonstrated has shed some light on the problems of painting animals and pets in watercolour. I hope too that your enthusiasm has grown, and also your confidence in your ability to embark on an admittedly taxing but nevertheless rewarding subject, full of interest and variety. What is most important fundamentally is to approach every painting as one that is totally different from any done in the past; when you paint an animal you are in effect painting a portrait, with the same obligations of careful consideration and understanding of the subject as with a human portrait.

Every individual animal is a little different from the rest of its species, just as every individual homo sapiens is a little different from any other. It is, however, necessary to be familiar with the variety to be able to recognise the differences. It has often been said, as though the fact suggested some mysterious power, that a shepherd can tell each sheep in his flock from all the others, but it is not considered remarkable for a school-master to be able to tell one boy from another, or for a television watcher to distinguish between actors – they even recognise them in disguise, and these are people they may never have seen in the flesh.

There is no mystery; if you are in a room with two dogs of the same breed, or two short-haired black cats, and start to draw them, you will immediately begin to see the differences between the two, and soon they will become two individuals to you. If you try the same thing with sheep, you will see differences between them also. As long as you maintain an attitude of interested enquiry, every subject you embark on will be new and different, and you will have found a source of unending pleasure and fascination.

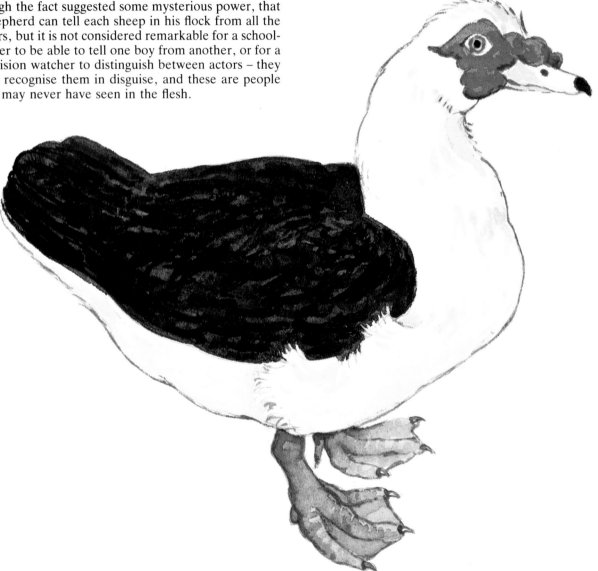